MW01285156

EVERYDAY
Literacy
Math

GRADE
PreK

Download Home–School Activities in Spanish

The Home–School Connection at the end of each weekly lesson in the book is also available in Spanish on our website.

How to Download:

1. Go to www.evan-moor.com/resources.

2. Enter your e-mail address and the resource code for this product—EMC3037.

3. You will receive an e-mail with a link to the downloadable letters, as well as an attachment with instructions.

Writing: Camille Liscinsky
Guadalupe Lopez
Content Editing: Guadalupe Lopez
Lisa Vitarisi Mathews
Copy Editing: Cathy Harber
Art Direction: Cheryl Puckett
Art Coordination: Kathy Kopp
Cover Design: Marcia Bateman
Illustration: Cheryl Nobens
Design/Production: Carolina Caird

EMC 3037

Evan-Moor
EDUCATIONAL PUBLISHERS
Helping Children Learn since 1979

Visit
teaching-standards.com
to view a correlation
of this book.
This is a free service.

**Correlated
to State Standards**

Contents

What's Inside

In this book, you will find **20 weekly lessons**. Each weekly lesson includes:

3 Teacher Pages

Use these pages to guide you through the week.

A script to follow that introduces the math concept

A short story to read aloud to children

Daily discussion questions about the story and math concept, plus a script to guide children through the activities

An activity that reinforces the weekly math concept

Samples of children's expected responses

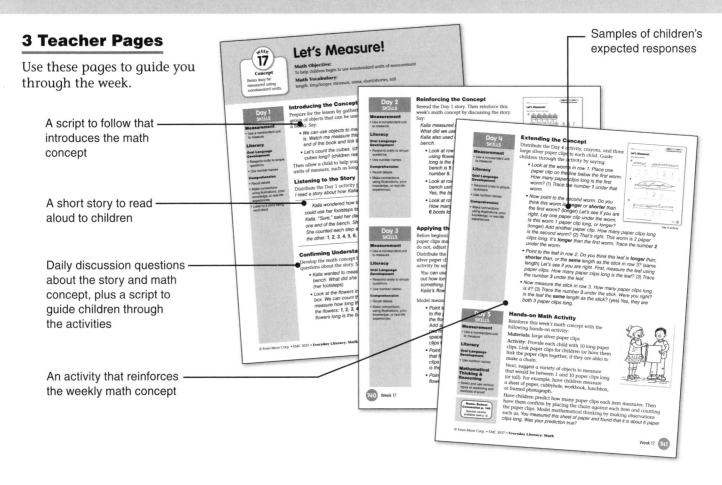

4 Student Activity Pages

Reproduce each page for children to complete during the daily lesson.

1 Home–School Connection Page

At the end of each week, give children the **Home–School Connection** page (in English or Spanish) to take home and share with their parents.

To access the Spanish version of the page, go to www.evan-moor.com/resources. Enter your e-mail address and the resource code EMC3037.

How to Use This Book

Follow these easy steps to conduct the lessons:

Day 1

Reproduce and distribute the *Day 1 Student Page* to each child.

Use the scripted *Day 1 Teacher Page* to:

1. Introduce the weekly concept.

2. Read the story aloud as children listen and look at the picture.

3. Guide children through the activity.

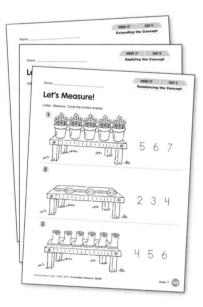

Days 2, 3, and 4

Reproduce and distribute the appropriate day's activity page to each child.

Use the scripted *Teacher Page* to:

1. Discuss the Day 1 story and reinforce the math concept.

2. Practice or extend the math concept.

3. Guide children through the activity

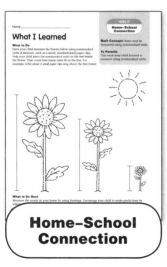

Home–School Connection

Day 5

Follow the directions to lead the *Math Activity*.

Send home the **Home–School Connection** page for each child to complete with his or her parents.

Tips for Success

• Review the *Teacher Page* before you begin the lesson.

• Work with children in small groups at a table in a quiet area of the room.

• Model how to respond to questions by using complete sentences. For example, if a child responds to the question "How many flowers long is the wall?" by answering "8," you'd respond, "That's right. The wall is 8 flowers long."

• Wait for children to complete each task before giving the next direction.

• Provide visual aids or concrete demonstrations when possible.

Skills Chart

	Math																				
	Number Sense												Data Analysis	Algebra				Geometry			
Week	Show an understanding of the quantity of one	Match objects from two groups using one-to-one correspondence	Apply one-to-one correspondence while counting	Understand the relationship between numbers and quantities	Understand that the final number counted in a set tells how many	Recognize the symbols that represent numbers	Associate each number with one name	Compare relationships between quantities	Identify relative place or position of objects in a sequence	Understand that subtraction is *taking from*	Understand that addition is *adding to*	Use numbers and counting to solve word problems	Collect, organize, and record data	Recognize and form simple patterns through different modalities	Recognize a qualitative property, or attribute	Sort objects using a variety of attributes	Discriminate like and unlike items	Recognize simple shapes, regardless of size or orientation	Recognize geometric shapes in the environment	Compare basic shapes by their attributes	Recognize and describe the spatial relationship between objects
1	•	•																			
2														•							
3			•	•	•																
4			•	•		•	•														
5																		•	•		
6																		•	•	•	
7			•		•										•	•					
8																	•				
9																					•
10																					
11			•	•		•	•														
12			•			•	•														
13		•							•												
14	•				•						•										
15	•				•					•											
16																			•		
17																					
18									•												
19												•									
20			•										•								

Everyday Literacy: Math • EMC 3037 • © Evan-Moor Corp.

Measurement			Mathematical Thinking and Reasoning					Oral Language Development					Comprehension					Week
Recognize the properties of length, size, and weight	Understand basic time concepts	Use a nonstandard unit to measure	Use number concepts for a meaningful purpose	Use math to solve problems	Use patterning to develop a sense of sequence	Explore mathematical ideas through song or play	Select and use various types of reasoning and methods of proof	Respond orally to simple questions	Use mathematical terms	Use the names of basic shapes	Use number names	Use vocabulary related to time concepts	Recall details	Make connections using illustrations, prior knowledge, or real-life experiences	Listen to a story being read aloud	Make inferences and draw conclusions	Understand how mathematical ideas build on one another	
			•	•				•			•		•	•	•	•		1
					•			•	•				•	•	•			2
						•		•			•		•	•	•			3
						•		•			•		•	•	•			4
						•		•		•			•	•	•			5
							•	•		•			•	•	•	•		6
				•				•	•		•		•	•	•		•	7
				•		•		•	•				•	•	•	•		8
						•		•	•		•		•	•	•			9
	•					•		•				•	•	•	•	•		10
						•		•			•		•	•	•			11
						•		•			•		•	•	•	•		12
						•		•	•				•	•	•			13
						•		•			•		•	•	•			14
						•		•			•		•	•	•	•		15
•							•	•	•	•			•	•	•	•		16
		•					•	•			•		•	•	•			17
						•		•			•		•	•	•	•		18
				•				•	•		•		•	•	•			19
							•	•			•		•	•	•			20

Everyday Literacy
Math

Student Progress Record

Name: _____

Write dates and comments in the boxes below the student's proficiency level.

1: Rarely demonstrates   0 – 25%
2: Occasionally demonstrates   25 – 50%
3: Usually demonstrates   50 – 75%
4: Consistently demonstrates   75 – 100%

Pre-Literacy Concepts	1	2	3	4
Communicates using drawing and tracing				
Tracks print and pictures from left to right and top to bottom				
Understands that pictures and symbols have meaning and that print carries a message				

Oral Language Development				
Uses descriptive language				
Responds orally to simple questions				

Comprehension				
Recalls details				
Makes connections using illustrations, prior knowledge, or real-life experiences				
Listens to stories being read aloud				
Makes inferences and draws conclusions				

Math				
Uses mathematical terms when speaking				
Engages in mathematical thinking and reasoning				
Applies mathematical concepts in written practice activities				

PreK

8

Everyday Literacy
Math

Small-Group Record Sheet

Students' Names:

Write dates and comments about students' performance each week.

Week	Title	Comments
1	One to One	
2	Find the Pattern	
3	Count to 5	
4	Find the Numbers	
5	Basic Shapes	
6	Compare Shapes	
7	Sort and Classify	
8	Does It Belong?	
9	Where Is It?	
10	Time of Day	
11	Count to 10	
12	What's the Number?	
13	More or Less	
14	One More	
15	Take Away One	
16	How Are They Different?	
17	Let's Measure!	
18	First in Line	
19	Find the Answer	
20	Graphs	

Dear Parent or Guardian,

Every week your child will learn a math concept related to number sense, geometry, data analysis, measurement, or algebra. Your child will develop oral language and comprehension skills by listening to stories and engaging in oral, written, and hands-on activities that reinforce math concepts.

At the end of each week, I will send home an activity page for you to complete with your child. The activity page reviews the weekly math concept and has an activity for you and your child to do together.

Sincerely,

Estimado padre o tutor:

Cada semana su niño(a) aprenderá sobre un concepto de matemáticas relacionado a la noción de los números, geometría, análisis de datos, medidas o álgebra. Su niño(a) desarrollará las habilidades de lenguaje oral y de comprensión escuchando cuentos y realizando actividades orales y escritas. Además, participará en actividades prácticas que apoyan los conceptos de matemáticas.

Al final de cada semana, le enviaré una hoja de actividades para que la complete en casa con su niño(a). La hoja repasa el concepto de matemáticas de la semana, y contiene una actividad que pueden completar usted y su niño(a) juntos.

Atentamente,

One to One

Math Objective:
To introduce children to the concept of one-to-one correspondence

Math Vocabulary:
count, each, enough, one

Number Sense

• Show an understanding of the quantity of one

• Match objects from two groups using one-to-one correspondence

Literacy

Oral Language Development

• Respond orally to simple questions

• Use number names

Comprehension

• Recall details

• Make connections using illustrations, prior knowledge, or real-life experiences

• Listen to a story being read aloud

• Make inferences and draw conclusions

Introducing the Concept

Model one-to-one correspondence. Distribute one crayon to each child. Say:

I gave one crayon to each of you. Count how many crayons you have.
*(1) Yes, the number **1** tells how many crayons you each have.*

Listening to the Story

Distribute the Day 1 activity page to each child. Say: *Listen and look at the picture as I read a story about some pandas who each have one chair and one cookie.*

Once upon a time, there were three pandas: Papa Panda, Mama Panda, and Baby Panda. They lived in a cozy house in the forest. Each panda had one chair. Papa Panda sat in the great big chair. Mama Panda sat in the medium-sized chair. And Baby Panda sat in the little bitty chair. Each panda ate one cookie. Papa Panda ate a great big cookie. Mama Panda ate a medium-sized cookie. And Baby Panda ate a little bitty cookie. After eating their cookies, the three pandas got into one big bed and went to sleep.

Confirming Understanding

Distribute crayons. Develop the math concept by asking children questions about the story. Say:

Day 1 picture

• *There are 3 pandas. Why are there 3 chairs?* (Each panda has 1 chair.)

• *Let's count the panda in the big chair.* (1) *Make a blue dot on the big chair.*

• *Let's count the panda in the medium-sized chair.* (1) *Make a red dot on the medium-sized chair.*

• *Let's count the panda in the little bitty chair.* (1) *Make a green dot on the little bitty chair.*

• *Now let's count Papa Panda's cookie.* (1) Repeat the process for Mama Panda and Baby Panda.

• *What happened at the end of the story?* (students respond) *Yes, 3 pandas got into 1 bed.*

Number Sense

- Show an understanding of the quantity of one
- Match objects from two groups using one-to-one correspondence

Literacy

Oral Language Development

- Respond orally to simple questions
- Use number names

Comprehension

- Recall details
- Make connections using illustrations, prior knowledge, or real-life experiences

Reinforcing the Concept

Reread the Day 1 story. Then reinforce this week's math concept by modeling one-to-one correspondence. Hold up one finger each time you say "one chair." Say:

Our story was about Papa Panda, Mama Panda, and Baby Panda. Papa Panda sat in 1 chair. Mama Panda sat in 1 chair. How many chairs did Baby Panda sit in? (1)

Distribute the Day 2 activity and crayons. Say:

- *Point to the great big chair. Who sat in the great big chair? (Papa Panda) With your finger, follow the line from the great big chair to Papa Panda.*
- *Point to the medium-sized chair. Who sat in the medium-sized chair? (Mama Panda) With your finger, follow the line from the medium-sized chair to Mama Panda.*
- *Point to the little bitty chair. Who sat in the little chair? (Baby Panda) With your finger, follow the line from the little chair to Baby Panda.*
- *Now use a crayon to trace the line from each chair to each panda.*

Day 2 activity

Number Sense

- Show an understanding of the quantity of one
- Match objects from two groups using one-to-one correspondence

Literacy

Oral Language Development

- Respond orally to simple questions
- Use number names

Comprehension

- Make connections using illustrations, prior knowledge, or real-life experiences
- Make inferences and draw conclusions

Applying the Concept

Distribute the Day 3 activity and crayons. Then introduce the activity by saying:

Mama Panda bought cookies from the bakery. Do you think there are enough cookies for everyone in the Panda family? (yes) Let's give each panda 1 cookie.

- *Put your crayon on Papa Panda. Draw a line from Papa Panda to 1 cookie.*
- *Put your crayon on Mama Panda. Draw a line from Mama Panda to 1 cookie.*
- *Put your crayon on Baby Panda. Draw a line from Baby Panda to 1 cookie.*

After children finish, ask:

- *Were there enough cookies for everyone in the Panda family? (yes)*
- *How many cookies did you give each panda? (1)*

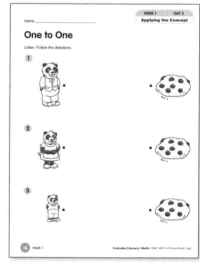

Day 3 activity

Number Sense

- Show an understanding of the quantity of one
- Match objects from two groups using one-to-one correspondence

Literacy

Oral Language Development

- Respond orally to simple questions

Comprehension

- Make connections using illustrations, prior knowledge, or real-life experiences

Extending the Concept

Distribute the Day 4 activity and crayons. Introduce the activity by saying:

It's time for cookies and milk! Each cookie needs one carton of milk.

- *Put your crayon on a chocolate chip cookie. Draw a line from that cookie to a carton of milk. Do the same for the other cookie. Are there enough cartons of milk? Color the happy face for **yes** or the sad face for **no**.* (yes)
- *Put your crayon on a sugar cookie. Draw a line from that cookie to a carton of milk. Do the same for the other cookies. Are there enough cartons of milk? Color the happy face for **yes** or the sad face for **no**.* (yes)
- *Put your crayon on a teddy bear cookie. Draw a line from that cookie to a carton of milk. Do the same for the other cookie. Are there enough cartons of milk? Color the happy face for **yes** or the sad face for **no**.* (no)
- *Put your crayon on a chocolate sandwich cookie. Draw a line from that cookie to a carton of milk. Do the same for the other cookies. Are there enough cartons of milk? Color the happy face for **yes** or the sad face for **no**.* (yes)

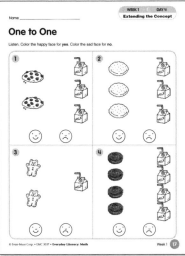

Day 4 activity

Number Sense

- Match objects from two groups using one-to-one correspondence

Mathematical Thinking & Reasoning

- Use number concepts for a meaningful purpose
- Use math to solve problems

Home–School Connection p. 18
Spanish version available (see p. 2)

Hands-on Math Activity

Reinforce this week's math concept with the following hands-on activity:

Materials: cookies, plates, napkins

Activity: Place children in groups of four. Model one-to-one correspondence by distributing one napkin to each child in the first group, counting as you set each napkin down. Say: *1, 2, 3, 4. Four napkins for four children.* Have one child from each group distribute the napkins in the same manner.

Then say: *Today we will do a math problem using cookies. I will give a plate of cookies to each group. Each group will share the plate of cookies, and each child will get one cookie. Groups may have to work together to make sure everyone gets a cookie.* Place a plate of cookies in the center of each group. Each plate should have either 3, 4, or 5 cookies. Model mathematical thinking by posing questions such as, *Do you have enough cookies?* (Answers will vary.) *How can you find out?* (by counting)

Have one child from each group tell how he or she solved the problem of distributing the cookies equally.

Name _____

One to One

Everyday Literacy: Math • EMC 3037 • © Evan-Moor Corp.

Name _____

One to One

Listen. Follow the directions.

Name _____

One to One

Listen. Follow the directions.

1

 •   •

2

 •   •

3

 •   •

Name _____

One to One

Listen. Color the happy face for **yes**. Color the sad face for **no**.

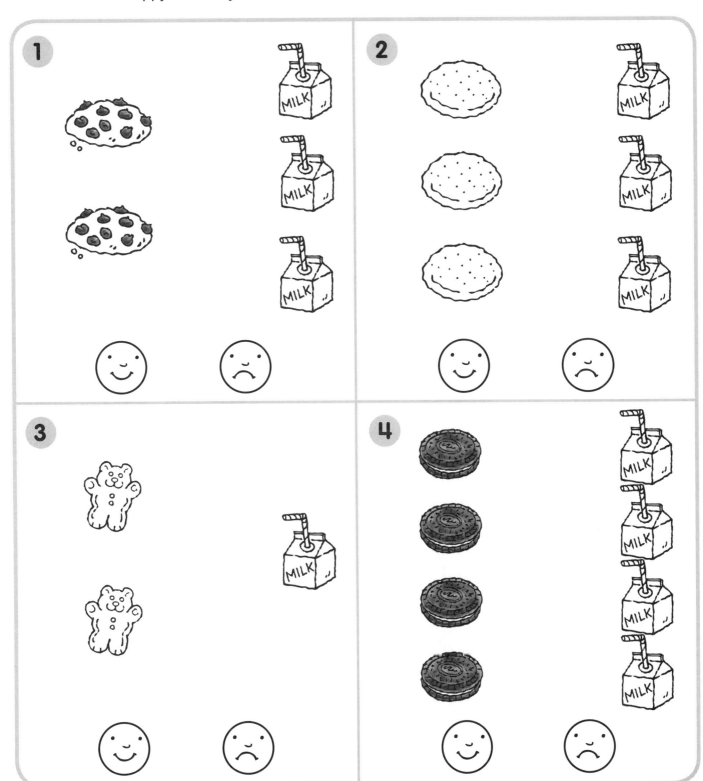

Name _____

What I Learned

What to Do
Look at the pictures below with your child. Talk about the number of chairs and the number of pandas. Have your child show you how to match one chair to each panda. Then ask your child to draw one cookie for each panda.

Math Concept: One-to-one correspondence is a basis for counting.

To Parents
This week your child learned to use one-to-one correspondence.

What to Do Next
Practice one-to-one correspondence while performing everyday activities. At dinnertime, for example, ask your child to set one napkin at each place setting. Help him or her count aloud each napkin as it is being set down.

Everyday Literacy: Math • EMC 3037 • © Evan-Moor Corp.

Find the Pattern

Math Objective:
To help children recognize, extend, and predict simple patterns

Math Vocabulary:
extend, group, pattern, predict, repeat

Day 1
SKILLS

Algebra
- Recognize and form simple patterns through different modalities

Literacy

Oral Language Development
- Respond orally to simple questions
- Use mathematical terms

Comprehension
- Make connections using illustrations, prior knowledge, or real-life experiences
- Listen to a story being read aloud

Introducing the Concept

Begin the lesson by modeling patterns. Display several colored blocks or other objects in an AB pattern (e.g., blue, red, blue, red). Point to each object as you explain the idea of a pattern. Say:

Look at these objects: blue, red, blue, red. The objects form a pattern. A pattern is a group of objects that repeats. Let's say the repeating pattern together: **blue, red**.

Repeat the process with a more complex AABB pattern, such as blue, blue, red, red.

Listening to the Story

Distribute the Day 1 activity page to children. Say: *This is Old MacDonald. These animals are on Old MacDonald's farm. The animals form patterns. Look for the patterns while I read the story.*

Old MacDonald had a farm. Ee-i-ee-i-o! And on that farm he had some pigs. Big pig, baby pig; big pig, baby pig. Ee-i-ee-i-o! Old MacDonald had a farm. And on that farm he had some cows and sheep. Cow, cow, sheep; cow, cow, sheep. Ee-i-ee-i-o! Old MacDonald had a farm. And on that farm he had some birds. Chick, chick, duck, duck; chick, chick, duck, duck. Old MacDonald had a farm. Ee-i-ee-i-o!

Confirming Understanding

Distribute crayons. Develop the math concept by asking questions about the story. Say:

Day 1 picture

- *Look at the cows and sheep. Do you see a pattern?* (yes) *What is the pattern?* (cow, cow, sheep) *Make a black dot on each cow.*

- *Look at the pigs. Do the pigs form a pattern?* (yes) *What is the pattern?* (big pig, baby pig) *Make a big dot on each big pig.*

- *Look at the birds. Do the birds form a pattern?* (yes) *What is it?* (chick, chick, duck, duck) *Point to each animal as you say "cheep" for each chick and "quack" for each duck.* (cheep, cheep, quack, quack, etc.)

Algebra

• Recognize and form simple patterns through different modalities

Literacy

Oral Language Development

• Respond orally to simple questions

Comprehension

• Recall details

• Make connections using illustrations, prior knowledge, or real-life experiences

Reinforcing the Concept

Reread the Day 1 story. Then reinforce this week's math concept by guiding a discussion about the story. Say:

Old MacDonald had cows and sheep on his farm. They were lined up in a cow, cow, sheep pattern. What other animals were lined up in a pattern? (pigs, birds)

Distribute the Day 2 activity and crayons. Say: *Here are more pictures from Old MacDonald's farm. Let's find the pattern for each group of pictures.*

Day 2 activity

• *Put your finger on the first chick. Point to each animal as we say its name together:* **chick, chick, pig; chick, chick, pig.** *What animal comes next,* **chick** *or* **pig**? (chick) *Draw a circle around the chick.*

• *Put your finger on the first sheep. Point to each animal as we say its name together:* **sheep, duck, duck; sheep, duck, duck.** *What animal comes next,* **duck** *or* **sheep**? (sheep) *That's right. Draw a circle around the sheep.*

• *Put your finger on the first dog. Point to each animal as we say its name together:* **dog, dog, cat, cat; dog, dog.** *What animal comes next,* **cat** *or* **dog**? (cat) *Draw a circle around the cat.*

Algebra

• Recognize and form simple patterns through different modalities

Literacy

Oral Language Development

• Respond orally to simple questions

Comprehension

• Make connections using illustrations, prior knowledge, or real-life experiences

Applying the Concept

Distribute the Day 3 activity and crayons. Then introduce the activity by saying:

• *Point to the first sheep. Let's find the pattern. Point to each sheep as we read:* **gray sheep, white sheep; gray sheep, white sheep.** *What color should the next sheep be?* (gray) *Color the sheep gray.*

• *Point to the first cat. Let's find the pattern. Point to each cat as we read:* **white cat, gray cat, gray cat; white cat, gray cat, gray cat; white cat, gray cat.** *What color should the next cat be?* (gray) *Color the cat gray.*

Day 3 activity

Repeat the process for white chick, white chick, gray chick, gray chick and white rabbit, gray rabbit, black rabbit. After children finish coloring each row of patterns, name the completed patterns aloud.

Algebra

• Recognize and form simple patterns through different modalities

Literacy

Oral Language Development

• Respond orally to simple questions

Comprehension

• Make connections using illustrations, prior knowledge, or real-life experiences

Extending the Concept

Introduce the activity by explaining to children that they can also create a pattern by using sounds. And they can repeat, or extend, it. Say:

We can create a pattern using sounds. We can use our hands and our feet. Watch and listen.

Stand up and model a clap-clap-stomp pattern. Then say:

Now you stand up and do the clap-clap-stomp pattern. Keep going until I say "Stop!"

Distribute the Day 4 activity and crayons. Say:

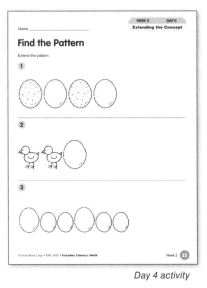

Day 4 activity

• *Look at the eggs. These are speckled eggs and white eggs. Let's find the pattern. Point to each egg as we name it:* **speckled egg**, **white egg**; **speckled egg**, **white egg**. *Now draw more eggs to extend the pattern. Draw a* **speckled** *egg first. Then draw a* **white** *egg.*

• *Now look at the chicks and egg. Point to each item as we name it:* **chick**, **chick**, **egg**. *What is the pattern?* (chick, chick, egg) *Extend the pattern. Draw* **chick**, **chick**, **egg**.

• *Now point to the next pattern. What does this pattern have?* (big eggs and little eggs) *Let's name the pattern. Point to each egg as we name it:* **big egg**, **little egg**, **little egg**; **big egg**, **little egg**, **little egg**. *What is the pattern?* (big egg, little egg, little egg) *Draw more eggs to extend the pattern one more time.*

Algebra

• Recognize and form simple patterns through different modalities

Mathematical Thinking & Reasoning

• Use patterning to develop a sense of sequence

Home–School Connection p. 26
Spanish version available (see p. 2)

Hands-on Math Activity

Reinforce this week's math concept with the following hands-on activity:

Materials: red, yellow, and green paper squares

Activity: Have children sit in a horizontal line. Place a pile of red, yellow, and green paper squares in front of the line where all children can access them. Make sure the colored squares are shuffled and slightly scattered.

Display an AB pattern for children to follow, for example: red square, yellow square, red square, yellow square.

Point to the pattern and ask: *What is the pattern here?* (red, yellow) *Let's make the same pattern using these paper squares.*

Ask the first child in line to take a red square and place it on the floor in front of him or her. Have children predict what color comes next (yellow), and invite the next child to choose and place the correct square. Continue extending the pattern until all children have a colored square in front of them. Then repeat the activity using a different pattern.

Name _____

Find the Pattern

Everyday Literacy: Math • EMC 3037 • © Evan-Moor Corp.

Name _____

Find the Pattern

Listen. Circle what comes **next**.

Find the Pattern

Color to complete the pattern.

 1

2

3

4

Name _____

Find the Pattern

Extend the pattern.

1

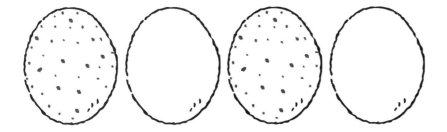

2

3

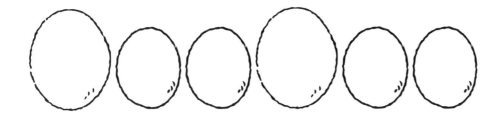

Name _____

What I Learned

What to Do
Have your child look at the picture below. Have him or her point to animals that are arranged in patterns. Then ask your child to have each animal in the pattern represent a different sound. For example, *cow, cow, sheep* could mean *moo, moo, baa,* or something entirely different!

WEEK 2

Home–School Connection

Math Concept: A pattern is a group of items that repeats.

To Parents
This week your child learned to recognize and extend patterns.

What to Do Next
Look for patterns all around your home, such as in floor tiles or wall decorations. Encourage your child to create new patterns with everyday items, such as lining up fork, spoon, fork, spoon.

Everyday Literacy: Math • EMC 3037 • © Evan-Moor Corp.

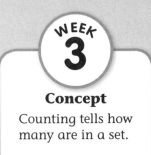

Concept

Counting tells how many are in a set.

Count to 5

Math Objective:

To help children count 5 or fewer items in a set

Math Vocabulary:

one, two, three, four, five, count, group, how many, order

Day 1 SKILLS

Number Sense

- Apply one-to-one correspondence while counting
- Understand the relationship between numbers and quantities
- Understand that the final number counted in a set tells how many

Literacy

Oral Language Development

- Respond orally to simple questions
- Use number names

Comprehension

- Make connections using illustrations, prior knowledge, or real-life experiences
- Listen to a story being read aloud

Introducing the Concept

Display sets of objects to count, such as blocks of the same shape or crayons of the same color. Have the sets equal any number from **1** to **5**. Point to each item as you say each number. For example, say:

I have some blocks. I want to know how many blocks there are, so I'm going to count them: 1, 2, 3, 4, 5. So let's count the blocks again. This time you count with me: 1, 2, 3, 4, 5.

Model counting another set of items in the same manner. Then place children in small groups and give each group a set of objects of 5 or fewer to count.

Listening to the Story

Distribute the Day 1 activity page to each child. Say: *Listen and look at the picture as I read a poem about animals. Listen as I count the animals.*

How many frogs like to dive?
1, 2, 3, 4, 5.

How many bees buzz at the hive?
1, 2, 3, 4, 5.

How many dogs want to drive?
1, 2, 3, 4, 5.

It's fun to count to five!

Confirming Understanding

Distribute crayons. Develop the math concept of counting to 5. Say:

- *I want to know how many frogs are ready to dive into the water. Watch me make a dot with my crayon on each frog as I count it: 1, 2, 3, 4, 5. Now let's count the frogs together. Make a dot on each frog as you count: 1, 2, 3, 4, 5.*

- *How many dogs want to drive? (5) Make a dot on each dog as you count: 1, 2, 3, 4, 5.*

- *I see other animals in this picture, too. I see fish and a cat. How many fish are there? (3) Color the fish orange.*

- *How many cats are there? (1) Color the cat brown.*

- *How many bees are there? (5) Color the bees yellow.*

Day 1 picture

Number Sense

- Apply one-to-one correspondence while counting

- Understand the relationship between numbers and quantities

Literacy

Oral Language Development

- Respond orally to simple questions

- Use number names

Comprehension

- Recall details

- Make connections using illustrations, prior knowledge, or real-life experiences

Reinforcing the Concept

Reinforce this week's math concept by discussing the Day 1 poem. Say:

What was the poem about? (animals, counting) *How many frogs did we count?* (5)

Distribute the Day 2 activity and crayons. Say:

- *Look at the cats. How can we find out how many cats there are?* (count) *Let's count the cats together. Make a black line under each cat as you count:* **1, 2, 3, 4, 5.**

- *Look at the fish. How can we find out how many fish there are?* (count) *Count the fish. Make an orange dot on each fish as you count:* **1, 2, 3, 4.**

- *Look at the dogs. How can we find out how many dogs there are?* (count) *Count the dogs. Make a brown dot on each dog as you count:* **1, 2, 3.**

- *Look at the bees. How can we find out how many bees there are?* (count) *Count the bees. Make a yellow line under each bee as you count:* **1, 2.**

- *Look at the frog. How can we find out how many frogs there are?* (count) *Count the frogs. Make a green dot on each frog as you count:* **1.**

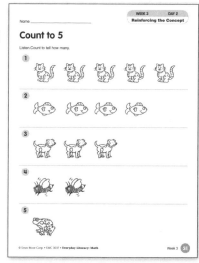

Day 2 activity

Number Sense

- Apply one-to-one correspondence while counting

- Understand the relationship between numbers and quantities

- Understand that the final number counted in a set tells how many

Literacy

Oral Language Development

- Respond orally to simple questions

- Use number names

Comprehension

- Make connections using illustrations, prior knowledge, or real-life experiences

Applying the Concept

Introduce the activity by saying:

Yesterday I read you a poem about counting. What did we count? (animals) *Yes, we counted 5 frogs, 5 bees, and 5 dogs. Now we're going to count other things to see if there are 5.*

Distribute the Day 3 activity and crayons. Say:

- *Look at the butterflies. Count them. Point to each one as you count.* (children count) *Are there* **5** *butterflies? Color the happy face for* **yes** *or the sad face for* **no.** (yes)

- *Look at the birds. Count them. Point to each one as you count.* (children count) *Are there* **5** *birds? Color the happy face for* **yes** *or the sad face for* **no.** (no) *How many birds are there?* (3)

- *Look at the rabbits. Count them. Point to each one as you count.* (children count) *Are there* **5** *rabbits? Color the happy face for* **yes** *or the sad face for* **no.** (no) *How many rabbits are there?* (2)

- *Look at the squirrels. Count them. Point to each one as you count.* (children count) *Are there* **5** *squirrels? Color the happy face for* **yes** *or the sad face for* **no.** (yes)

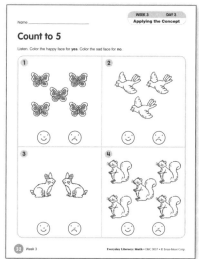

Day 3 activity

Number Sense

• Apply one-to-one correspondence while counting

• Understand the relationship between numbers and quantities

• Understand that the final number counted in a set tells how many

Literacy

Comprehension

• Make connections using illustrations, prior knowledge, or real-life experiences

Applying the Concept

Distribute the Day 4 activity and crayons. Say:

- *Look at the bees. There are two groups. Count the bees in each group. Point to each bee as you count it.* (children count) *Circle the group that has **3** bees.*

- *Look at the birds. Count the birds in each group. Point to each bird as you count it.* (children count) *Circle the group that has **4** birds.*

- *Look at the fish. Count the fish in each group. Point to each fish as you count it.* (children count) *Circle the group that has **5** fish.*

- *Look at the frogs. Count the frogs in each group. Point to each frog as you count it.* (children count) *Circle the group that has **1** frog.*

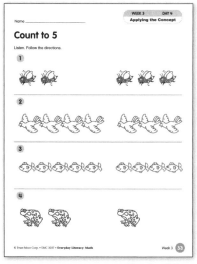

Day 4 activity

Number Sense

• Apply one-to-one correspondence while counting

Mathematical Thinking & Reasoning

• Explore mathematical ideas through song or play

Home–School Connection p. 34

Spanish version available (see p. 2)

Circle Time Math Activity

Reinforce this week's math concept with the following circle time activity, which is a variation of "Duck, Duck, Goose":

Have children sit cross-legged in a circle, facing each other. You be "It" (the Counter) for the first round so children understand the object of the game.

Walk around the circle tapping each child's head while counting aloud *1, 2, 3, 4, 5* over and over. Stop at any number to designate who will be "the Chaser."

The Chaser must jump up and chase the Counter around the circle, trying to tag him or her before the Counter sits at the Chaser's place in the circle.

If the Counter steals the Chaser's place in the circle before being tagged, the Chaser becomes the new Counter. If the Counter gets tagged, he or she remains the Counter for one more round. After that, assign a new Counter so that other children have the opportunity to count.

Name _____

Count to 5

    Everyday Literacy: Math • EMC 3037 • © Evan-Moor Corp.

Name _____

Count to 5

Listen. Count to tell how many.

1

2

3

4

5

Name _____

Count to 5

Listen. Color the happy face for **yes**. Color the sad face for **no**.

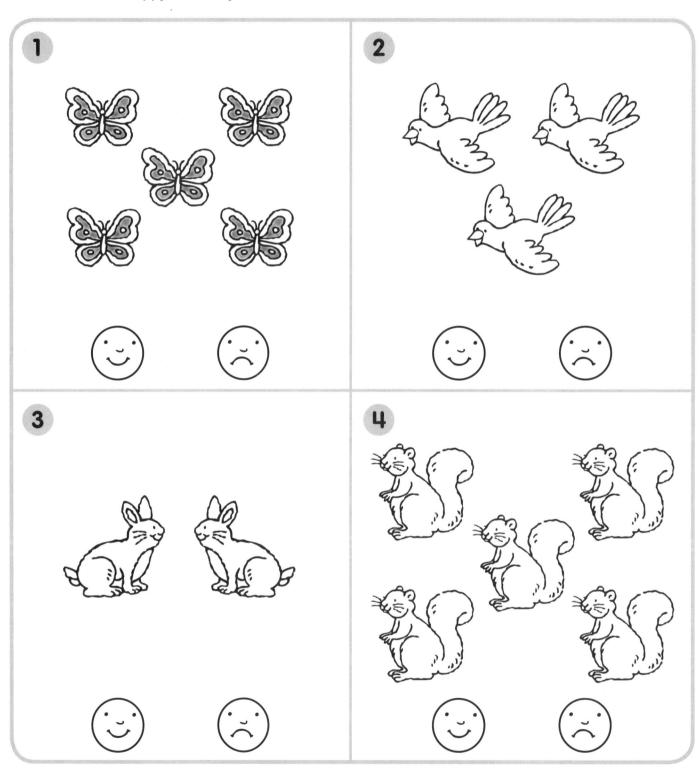

Name _____

Count to 5

Listen. Follow the directions.

Name _____

What I Learned

What to Do

Ask your child to tell what is happening in the picture. Then encourage him or her to count by asking questions such as, *How many fish are there? How many frogs? How many dogs?*

WEEK 3

Home–School Connection

Math Concept: Counting tells how many are in a set.

To Parents
This week your child learned to count to 5.

What to Do Next

Take a trip to the park and play "I Spy" with your child. When you spot small groups of countable items, say, *I spy some squirrels. How many squirrels are there?* Then let your child have a turn being the "spy."

Everyday Literacy: Math • EMC 3037 • © Evan-Moor Corp.

WEEK
4

Concept
Each number has a
name and a symbol.

Find the Numbers

Math Objective:
To help children recognize and name numbers 1 through 5

Math Vocabulary:
one, two, three, four, five

Day 1
SKILLS

Number Sense
• Apply one-to-one
correspondence while
counting

• Understand the
relationship between
numbers and quantities

• Recognize the symbols
that represent numbers

• Associate each number
with one name

Literacy

**Oral Language
Development**
• Respond orally to simple
questions

• Use number names

Comprehension
• Make connections
using illustrations, prior
knowledge, or real-life
experiences

• Listen to a story being
read aloud

Introducing the Concept

Before the lesson, make a number line that begins with number **1** and ends
with number **5**. Then display the number line. Say:

*These are the numbers **1** through **5**. Name them with me: **1**, **2**, **3**, **4**, **5**.
A number can tell how old you are. How old are you?* (children respond)

Next, trace each number with your finger and then have children use their
fingers to form each number in the air.

Listening to the Story

Distribute the Day 1 activity page to each child. Say: *I will read a poem to
you. Look at the picture and listen carefully. Some numbers are hiding here.*

---

*I see a **1** resting on my shoe.*
*Where, oh, where is the number **2**?*

*There is a **2** sticking to my knee!*
*Where, oh, where is the number **3**?*

*I see a **3** hanging on the door.*
*Where, oh, where is the number **4**?*

*There is a **4** learning how to drive!*
*Where, oh, where is the number **5**?*

*I see a **5** sizzling on the sun.*
*Now I'm back to number **1**.*

Confirming Understanding

Distribute crayons. Develop the math concept
by asking questions about the poem. Say:

Day 1 picture

• *Every number has a name: **1**, **2**, **3**, **4**, **5**.
Where do you see the number **1**?* (on
the shoe) *Trace the number **1** with blue.*

• *Where do you see the number **2**?* (on
her knee) *Trace the number **2** with red.*

• *Where do you see the number **3**?* (on
the door) *Trace the number **3** with green.*

• *Where do you see the number **4**?* (on the
car) *Trace the number **4** with orange.*

• *Where do you see the number **5**?* (on
the sun) *Trace the number **5** with yellow.*

• *Find the number that tells how old you are.
Draw a red circle around that number.*

Number Sense

• Recognize the symbols that represent numbers

Literacy

Oral Language Development

• Respond orally to simple questions

• Use number names

Comprehension

• Recall details

• Make connections using illustrations, prior knowledge, or real-life experiences

Reinforcing the Concept

Reread the Day 1 poem. Then reinforce this week's math concept. Say:

Our poem was about the numbers 1 through 5. Where was the number 2 hiding? (on the girl's knee) *Tell me where the other numbers were hiding.* (children respond)

Distribute the Day 2 activity and crayons. Say:

• *The girl lost her balloons. Help her find them. Point to the balloon with the number 1. Trace the number 1 with your finger.*

• *Point to the balloon with the number 2. Trace the number 2 with your finger.*

• *Point to the balloon with the number 3. Trace the 3 with your finger.*

• *Point to the balloon with the number 4. Trace the 4 with your finger.*

• *Point to the balloon with the number 5. Trace the 5 with your finger.*

• *Now that you have traced all the numbers with your finger, let's match the balloons. Find the balloon with the number 1. Draw a line to the other balloon with the number 1 on it.*

Repeat the process with the balloons numbered 2 through 5.

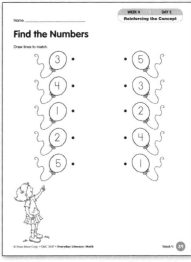

Day 2 activity

Number Sense

• Apply one-to-one correspondence while counting

• Understand the relationship between numbers and quantities

• Recognize the symbols that represent numbers

• Associate each number with one name

Literacy

Oral Language Development

• Respond orally to simple questions

• Use number names

Comprehension

• Make connections using illustrations, prior knowledge, or real-life experiences

Applying the Concept

To introduce the activity, say:

Remember that we use numbers to tell how many. How can we find out how many there are of something? (count)

Continue counting other sets of 5 or fewer. For example, ask: *How many fingers am I holding up? Let's count them: 1, 2, 3.*

Distribute the Day 3 activity and crayons. Say:

• *Put your finger on picture 1. It shows balloons. How can we find out how many balloons there are?* (count) *Count the balloons. How many balloons are there?* (4) *Circle the number 4.*

• *Put your finger on picture 2. It shows butterflies. How can we find out how many butterflies there are?* (count) *Count the butterflies. How many butterflies are there?* (3) *Circle the number 3.*

• *Put your finger on picture 3. It shows flowers. Count the flowers. How many flowers are there?* (5) *Circle the number 5.*

• *Put your finger on picture 4. It shows some shoes. Count the shoes. How many shoes are there?* (2) *Circle the number 2.*

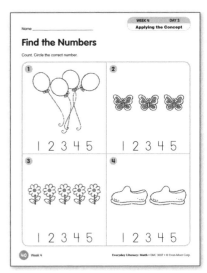

Day 3 activity

Everyday Literacy: Math • EMC 3037 • © Evan-Moor Corp.

WEEK 4   DAY 4
Extending the Concept

© Evan-Moor Corp. • EMC 3037 • **Everyday Literacy: Math**

Day 4 SKILLS

Number Sense

- Apply one-to-one correspondence while counting
- Understand the relationship between numbers and quantities
- Recognize the symbols that represent numbers
- Associate each number with one name

Literacy

Oral Language Development

- Respond orally to simple questions
- Use number names

Comprehension

- Make connections using illustrations, prior knowledge, or real-life experiences

Extending the Concept

Introduce the activity by reviewing the math concept. Say:

Each number has a name: 1, 2, 3, 4, 5. We write each number in a special way. Some numbers have curves. Others have lines, and some have both curves and lines. We use numbers to tell how many.

Distribute the Day 4 activity and crayons. Say:

- *Point to the ladybugs. How many ladybugs are there? (3) Draw a line from the ladybugs to the number 3. Now trace the number 3.*

- *Point to the sun. How many suns are there? (1) Draw a line from the sun to the number 1. Now trace the number 1.*

- *Point to the butterflies. How many butterflies are there? (2) Draw a line from the butterflies to the number 2. Now trace the number 2.*

- *Point to the flowers. How many flowers are there? (4) Draw a line from the flowers to the number 4. Now trace the number 4.*

- *Point to the bees. How many bees are there? (5) Draw a line from the bees to the number 5. Now trace the number 5.*

Name _____

Find the Numbers

Listen. Draw a line to match. Trace the number.

Day 4 activity

Day 5 SKILLS

Number Sense

- Apply one-to-one correspondence while counting
- Recognize the symbols that represent numbers

Mathematical Thinking & Reasoning

- Explore mathematical ideas through song or play

Home–School Connection p. 42
Spanish version available (see p. 2)

Circle Time Math Activity

Reinforce this week's math concept with the following circle time activity:

Materials: music player; a cardboard square for each child; pretzel sticks, raisins, or other small snack (Be aware of food allergies.)

Preparation: Number the cardboard squares from **1** to **5** several times over. Arrange them in a circular path for children to walk on. Alternatively, the numbers may be drawn on the playground with chalk.

Activity: Explain to children that they will play a game called "Number Walk." Have each child stand on a number square. Start the music, and tell children to walk on the number path while the music plays, making sure to stand on a number square each time they take a step. Stop the music. Call out a number from **1** to **5**. For example, if you call out the number **3**, whoever is standing on **3** wins three pretzel sticks (or other snack), which you enthusiastically count out as a class.

Name _____

Find the Numbers

Everyday Literacy: Math • EMC 3037 • © Evan-Moor Corp.

Name _____

Find the Numbers

Draw lines to match.

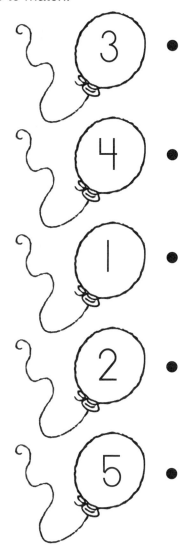

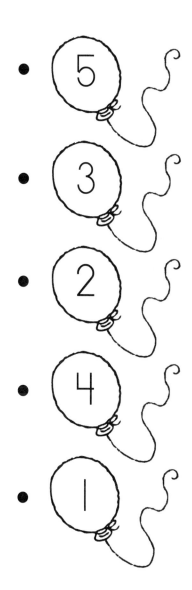

Name _____

Find the Numbers

Count. Circle the correct number.

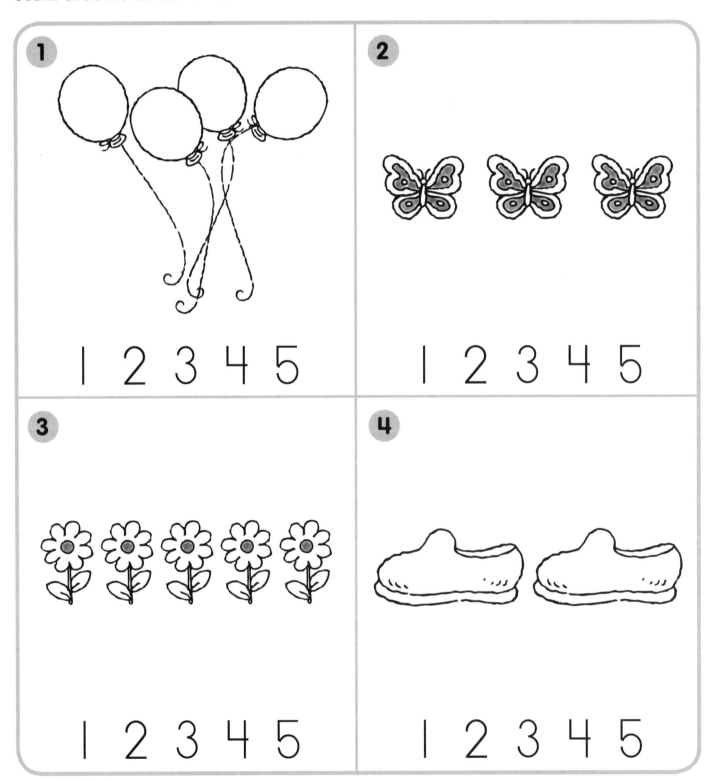

1

1 2 3 4 5

2

1 2 3 4 5

3

1 2 3 4 5

4

1 2 3 4 5

Everyday Literacy: Math • EMC 3037 • © Evan-Moor Corp.

Name _____

Find the Numbers

Listen. Draw a line to match. Trace the number.

 •   •

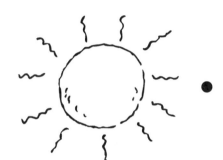 •   •

 •   •

 •   •

 •   • 5

Name _____

What I Learned

What to Do

Have your child look at the picture below. Ask him or her to count the balloons and tell you how many there are in one column. Then ask your child to name and match the numbers on the balloons. Finally, have your child color the picture.

WEEK 4

Home–School Connection

Math Concept: Each number has a name and a symbol.

To Parents
This week your child learned the names and symbols for 1–5.

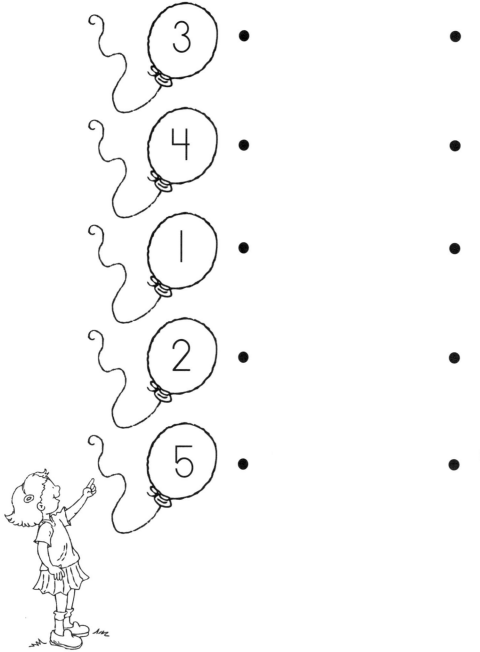

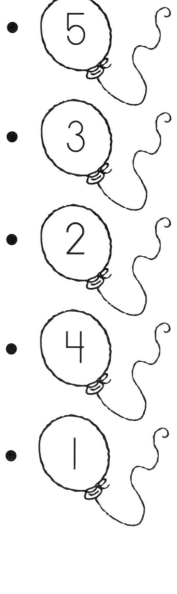

What to Do Next

Create sets of five or fewer items. Have your child tell you how many are in each set. Then help your child use self-stick notes to label each set with the correct number.

Everyday Literacy: Math • EMC 3037 • © Evan-Moor Corp.

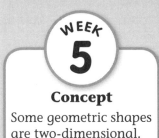

WEEK
5

Concept
Some geometric shapes
are two-dimensional.

Basic Shapes

Math Objective:
To help children identify and differentiate basic shapes

Math Vocabulary:
circle, flat, rectangle, round, shape, side, square, triangle

Day 1
SKILLS

Geometry
• Recognize simple
  shapes, regardless of
  size or orientation
• Recognize geometric
  shapes in the
  environment

Literacy

**Oral Language
Development**
• Respond orally to simple
  questions
• Use the names of basic
  shapes

Comprehension
• Recall details
• Make connections
  using illustrations, prior
  knowledge, or real-life
  experiences
• Listen to a story being
  read aloud

Introducing the Concept

Display four large shapes: a circle, a triangle, a rectangle, and a square. Then talk about each shape. Say:

- *This shape is round. It is called a circle. Say **circle**.* (circle)
- *This flat shape has three sides: **1**, **2**, **3**. It is called a triangle. Say **triangle**.* (triangle) *Now watch me flip the triangle. Is it still a triangle?* (yes) *I'm going to flip it again. Is it still a triangle?* (yes)

Repeat this process for the rectangle (four sides; two sides are long and two sides are short) and the square (four sides that are the same). Then ask children to point out shapes in the room.

Listening to the Story

Distribute the Day 1 activity page. Say: *I will read a story about a doll made of shapes. Listen to the story and point to each shape as I read about it.*

I have a paper doll named Suzy Shapey. You can see how Suzy got her name. She is made of shapes! Suzy Shapey's head is a circle. Her body is a big square. Her feet are little squares. Her legs are long rectangles. Do you see Suzy's purse? It is shaped like a triangle. I like the many shapes in Suzy Shapey!

Confirming Understanding

Distribute crayons. Reinforce the math concept about shapes. Ask:

- *Do you see a square on Suzy Shapey's face?* (yes) *Where?* (her nose) *Color her square nose pink.*
- *Suzy Shapey is holding a purse. What shape is it?* (triangle) *Color the triangle purple.*
- *What shape is Suzy Shapey's head?* (circle) *Find more circles.* (her hands) *Color all the circles yellow.*
- *Suzy Shapey's arms are rectangles. Color her arms red. What other body parts are shaped like rectangles?* (her legs) *Color her legs green.*

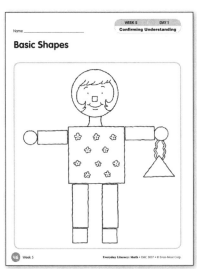

Day 1 picture

Geometry

- Recognize simple shapes, regardless of size or orientation

Literacy

Oral Language Development

- Respond orally to simple questions
- Use the names of basic shapes

Comprehension

- Recall details
- Make connections using illustrations, prior knowledge, or real-life experiences

Reinforcing the Concept

Reread the Day 1 story. Then reinforce this week's math concept by guiding a discussion about the story. Say:

Our story was about a paper doll named Suzy Shapey. Why is she named Suzy Shapey? (She is made of shapes.) What shape is Suzy Shapey's head? (circle)

Distribute the Day 2 activity and crayons. Say:

- *Point to box 1. Is this shape a circle? Color the happy face for **yes** or the sad face for **no**. (yes) Yes, a circle is round. Trace the circle with blue.*

- *Point to box 2. Is this shape a triangle? Color the happy face for **yes** or the sad face for **no**. (no) What shape is it? (square) How many sides does it have? (4) Trace the square with red.*

- *Point to box 3. Is this shape a rectangle? Color the happy face for **yes** or the sad face for **no**. (yes) How many sides does a rectangle have? (4) Yes, a rectangle has four sides: two short and two long. Trace the rectangle with green.*

- *Point to box 4. Is this shape a triangle? Color the happy face for **yes** or the sad face for **no**. (yes) How many sides does a triangle have? (3) Trace the triangle with purple.*

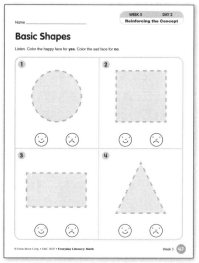

Day 2 activity

Geometry

- Recognize simple shapes, regardless of size or orientation
- Recognize geometric shapes in the environment

Literacy

Oral Language Development

- Respond orally to simple questions
- Use the names of basic shapes

Comprehension

- Recall details
- Make connections using illustrations, prior knowledge, or real-life experiences

Applying the Concept

Distribute the Day 3 activity and crayons. Say:

Look at the picture. It is made of shapes, just as Suzy Shapey was made of shapes.

- *Point to the house. The roof is a triangle. Color the triangle brown.*

- *What other shape do you see on the house? (square) Color the square blue.*

- *Look at the tree. It is made of two shapes. What are the two shapes? (rectangle and circle) Yes, the trunk of the tree is a rectangle. Color the rectangle brown. The top part is a circle. Color the circle green.*

- *Look at the sky. What shape do you see in the sky? (circle) Yes, the sun is a circle. Color the circle yellow.*

- *Look at the fence. What shapes do you see? (rectangles and triangles) Color the triangles blue. Color the rectangles orange.*

Day 3 activity

Geometry
- Recognize simple shapes, regardless of size or orientation

Literacy

Oral Language Development
- Respond orally to simple questions
- Use the names of basic shapes

Comprehension
- Make connections using illustrations, prior knowledge, or real-life experiences

Extending the Concept

Show a rectangle, triangle, square, and circle. Turn each shape in every direction; review that orientation does <u>not</u> change the shape:

Remember that a rectangle is a rectangle no matter which way it is turned.

Distribute the Day 4 activity and crayons. Say:

- *Point to the first triangle. It has 3 sides. Look at the other shapes in the row. Make a dot on the other triangle in this row. What are the other two shapes?* (circle and square)

- *Point to the rectangle. It has 2 short sides and 2 long sides. Look at the other shapes in the row. Make a dot on the other rectangle in this row. What are the other two shapes?* (triangle and square)

- *Point to the square. Look at the other shapes in this row. Make a dot on the square. What are the other shapes?* (circle and triangle)

- *Point to the circle. Look at the other shapes in this row. Make a dot on the circle. What are the other shapes?* (square and triangle)

Day 4 activity

Home–School Connection p. 50
Spanish version available (see p. 2)

Circle Time Math Activity

Reinforce this week's math concept with the following circle time activity:

Materials: triangle, circle, square, rectangle

Activity: Divide children into four groups. Assign each group a shape name. Appoint one child from each group as the leader, responsible for displaying the group's shape.

Children will march in a shape parade around the room. They should start marching when they hear their group's shape name.

Teach children this marching song (to the tune of "The Ants Go Marching One by One"):

(Chorus) *Let the shapes come marching in. Hoorah, hoorah!* (2x)
    Here's a triangle: 1, 2, 3. That's how many sides you'll see!
We'll all go marching in the shape parade! (Chorus)
    Here's a square: four sides the same. Hello, hello, we're glad you came!
We'll all go marching in the shape parade! (Chorus)
    Here's a rectangle with four sides. Two are short and two are wide.
We'll all go marching in the shape parade! (Chorus)
    Here's a circle. It's nice and round. Stomp your feet along the ground!
We'll all go marching in the shape parade! (Chorus)

Basic Shapes

Name _____

Basic Shapes

Listen. Color the happy face for **yes**. Color the sad face for **no**.

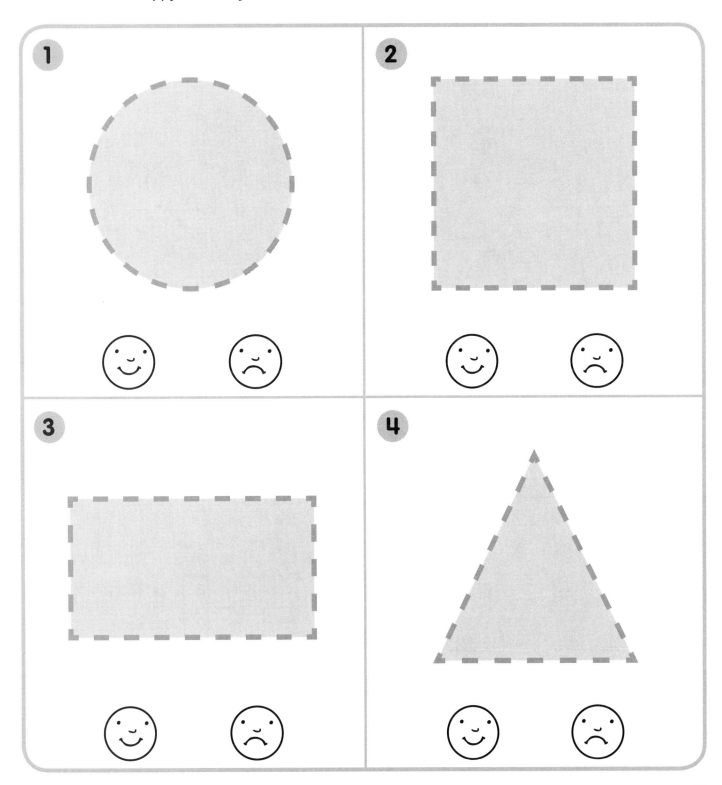

Name _____

Basic Shapes

Listen. Follow the directions.

Everyday Literacy: Math • EMC 3037 • © Evan-Moor Corp.

Name _____

Basic Shapes

Listen. Follow the directions.

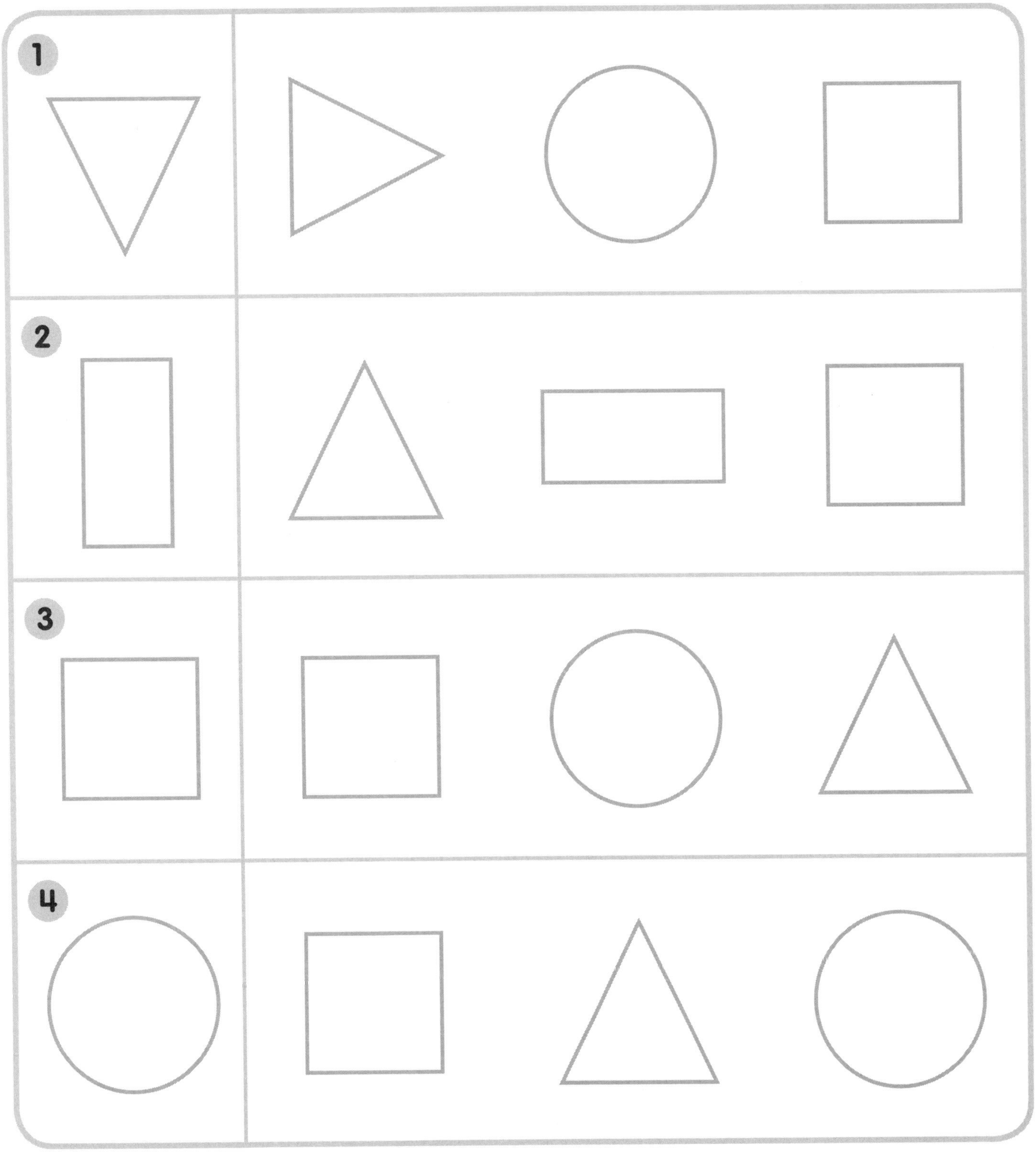

1

2

3

4

Name _____

What I Learned

What to Do
Have your child look at the picture below. Have him or her name
the different shapes hiding in the picture. Then have your child
follow the color key to color the picture.

△ green □ blue
○ red ▯ yellow

WEEK 5

Home–School Connection

Math Concept: Some
geometric shapes are
two-dimensional.

To Parents
This week your child learned
about basic shapes.

What to Do Next
Draw basic shapes on self-stick notes: circle, square, rectangle, triangle. Help your child search
around the house for these basic shapes, and have him or her label the items with the corresponding
self-stick note.

Compare Shapes

Math Objective:
To help children compare, describe, and draw shapes

Math Vocabulary:
circle, equal, long, rectangle, round, shape, short, sides, square, straight, triangle

Day 1
SKILLS

Geometry

• Recognize simple shapes, regardless of size or orientation

• Recognize geometric shapes in the environment

• Compare basic shapes by their attributes

Literacy

Oral Language Development

• Respond orally to simple questions

• Use the names of basic shapes

Comprehension

• Recall details

• Make connections using illustrations, prior knowledge, or real-life experiences

• Listen to a story being read aloud

• Make inferences and draw conclusions

Introducing the Concept

Prepare for the lesson by gathering a few circles, triangles, rectangles, and squares of different sizes. Show children the shapes as you describe them. Say:

These are shapes. Some are big and some are small. Let's name them: **circle**, **triangle**, **rectangle**, **square**. *Each shape is special. A triangle, a rectangle, and a square have sides. If I follow each side with my finger, I go in a straight line. Does a circle have sides?* (no) *No, a circle is round. If I follow the shape of the circle with my finger, it goes round and round.*

Repeat the process of describing a triangle (three sides), a rectangle (2 short sides and 2 long sides), and a square (four equal sides).

Listening to the Story

Distribute the Day 1 activity page to each child. Say: *Listen and look at the picture as I read a story about Robin and the shapes in her lunch.*

"Shapes are all around us," said Robin's teacher. "You can probably see shapes in your lunches." Was that true? Robin looked at her lunchbox. It had two long sides and two short sides. "My lunchbox is a rectangle," exclaimed Robin. "And my carrot sticks are rectangles, too!" She looked at her sandwich. Dad had cut the sandwich into two triangles. Robin smiled when she saw a cookie shaped like a circle. "I am going to enjoy eating this yummy shape!" said Robin.

Confirming Understanding

Distribute crayons. Develop the math concept by asking children questions about the story. Say:

Day 1 picture

• *Look at Robin's lunch. Her sandwich has two triangles. Where do you see a square?* (napkin) *How do you know that the napkin is a square?* (It has four equal sides.)

• *What did Robin eat that is round like a circle?* (cookie) *Trace around the cookie with brown.*

• *Are all rectangles the same size?* (no) *Which rectangle in the picture is the biggest?* (lunchbox) *Trace around the lunchbox with red.*

<table>
<tr><td>

Day 2
SKILLS

Geometry

- Recognize simple shapes, regardless of size or orientation
- Recognize geometric shapes in the environment
- Compare basic shapes by their attributes

Literacy

Oral Language Development

- Respond orally to simple questions
- Use the names of basic shapes

Comprehension

- Recall details
- Make inferences and draw conclusions

</td><td>

Reinforcing the Concept

Reread the Day 1 story. Then reinforce this week's math concept by discussing the story. Say:

In our story, Robin's lunchbox is a rectangle. Her carrot sticks are also rectangles. Robin's rectangles are different sizes. Are they still rectangles? (yes) That's right. A shape can be any size, big or small.

Distribute the Day 2 activity and crayons. Say:

- *Point to number 1. What shape is this? (triangle) How many sides does it have? (3) Draw a line to the shape that is also a triangle.*

- *Point to number 2. What shape is this? (square) How many sides does it have? (4) Are the sides the same? (yes) Draw a line to the bigger square. Does it also have 4 sides? (yes)*

- *Point to number 3. What shape is this? (rectangle) How many sides does it have? (4) Are the sides the same? (no) That's right, a rectangle has 2 long sides and 2 short sides. Draw a line to the smaller rectangle. Does it also have 2 long sides and 2 short sides? (yes)*

- *Point to number 4. What shape is this? (circle) Does it have sides like a square or a rectangle? (no) A circle has no sides. It is round. Draw a line to the other circle.*

</td></tr>
</table>

Day 2 activity

<table>
<tr><td>

Day 3
SKILLS

Geometry

- Recognize simple shapes, regardless of size or orientation
- Recognize geometric shapes in the environment
- Compare basic shapes by their attributes

Literacy

Oral Language Development

- Respond orally to simple questions

</td><td>

Applying the Concept

Distribute the Day 3 activity and crayons. Say:

- *Find the triangle at the bottom of the page. Trace the triangle with your finger. Find two triangles in the picture. What is shaped like triangles? (the sandwich) Trace the triangles in the sandwich with brown.*

- *Find the circle at the bottom of the page. Trace the circle with your finger. Find the circles in the picture. What are shaped like circles? (plates, pineapple, orange) Trace all the circles with red.*

- *Find the rectangle at the bottom. Trace it with your finger. Find a big rectangle in the picture. What is shaped like a rectangle? (placemat) Trace the placemat with blue.*

- *Find the square at the bottom. Trace it with your finger. Find four little squares in the picture. What are shaped like squares? (placemat corners) Color the squares green.*

</td></tr>
</table>

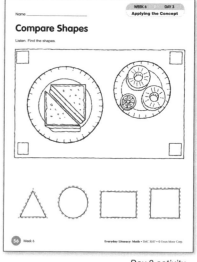

Day 3 activity

Everyday Literacy: Math • EMC 3037 • © Evan-Moor Corp.

Extending the Concept

Introduce the activity by displaying an AB pattern of circle, square, circle, square. Say:

Remember that a pattern is a group of items that repeats. What pattern do these shapes make? (circle, square)

Distribute the Day 4 activity and crayons. Say:

- *Put your finger on row 1. Remember that a shape can be any size. Point to each shape as we name it: **small circle**, **big circle**; **small circle**, **big circle**. What comes next?* (small circle, big circle) *Draw a small circle and a big circle.*

- *Put your finger on row 2. Point to each shape as we name it together: **rectangle**, **triangle**; **rectangle**, **triangle**. What comes next?* (rectangle, triangle) *Draw a rectangle and a triangle.*

- *Put your finger on row 3. Point to each shape as we name it together: **big square**, **little square**, **little square**; **big square**, **little square**, **little square**. What comes next?* (big square, little square, little square) *Draw a big square, a little square, and a little square.*

- *Put your finger on row 4. Point to each shape as we name it together: **circle**, **triangle**, **triangle**; **circle**, **triangle**, **triangle**. What comes next?* (circle, triangle, triangle) *Draw a circle, a triangle, and a triangle.*

Day 4 activity

Hands-on Math Activity

Reinforce this week's math concept with the following hands-on activity:

Materials: construction paper, glue, scissors, contact paper

Preparation: From the construction paper, cut out circles, squares, rectangles, and triangles of different sizes and colors.

Activity: Explain to children that they will be making shapes placemats. Divide children into small groups. Have each child choose a sheet of construction paper as the base of the placemat. Invite children to decorate their placemats by gluing shapes onto it. Emphasize that a shape can be any size; big or small, sideways or upright, a triangle is a triangle. Model mathematical thinking with observations such as, *I see a big yellow triangle here. I see a small blue triangle there. Are they both triangles?* (yes)

After children finish decorating their placemats, cover the placemats with contact paper or laminate them.

Name _____

Compare Shapes

Everyday Literacy: Math • EMC 3037 • © Evan-Moor Corp.

Name _____

Compare Shapes

Listen. Draw a line to match.

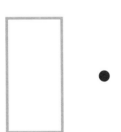 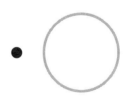

Name _____

Compare Shapes

Listen. Find the shapes.

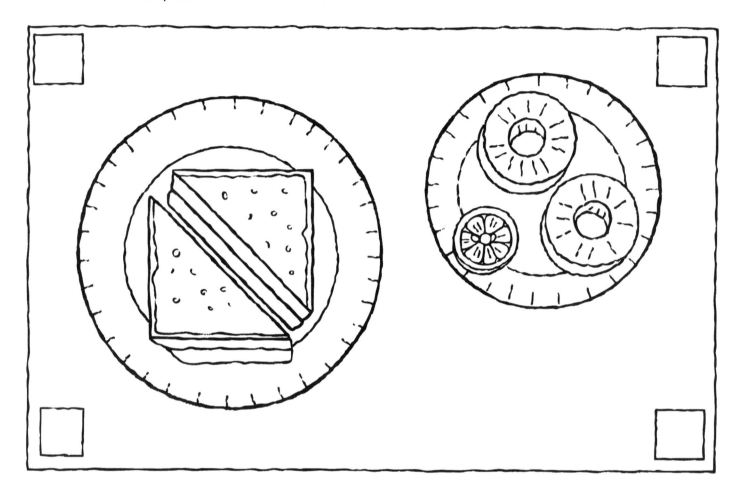

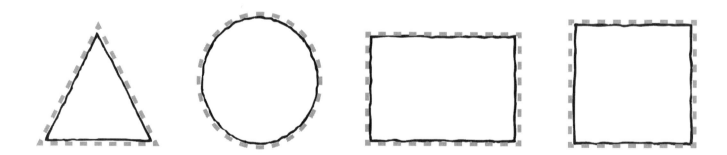

Everyday Literacy: Math • EMC 3037 • © Evan-Moor Corp.

Name _____

Compare Shapes

Draw the shapes that come next.

1

2

3

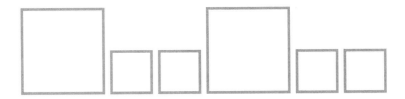

4

Name _____

What I Learned

What to Do
Have your child tell you the name of each shape at the bottom of the page. Then have him or her trace each shape. Next, have your child look at the picture below. Ask him or her to point to and name each shape in the picture.

WEEK 6
Home–School Connection

Math Concept: Shapes have attributes.

To Parents
This week your child compared basic shapes by their attributes.

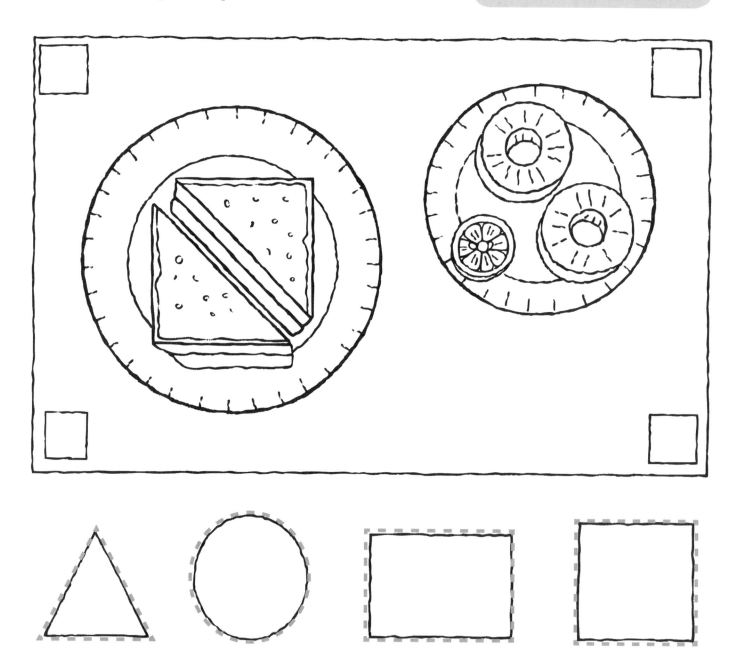

What to Do Next
Go on a shape walk with your child. Look for circles, squares, triangles, and rectangles along the way. For example, look at signs, traffic lights, sidewalks, and buildings.

Concept

Objects can be sorted into categories.

Sort and Classify

Math Objective:
To help children sort objects according to a variety of attributes

Math Vocabulary:
different, group, same, shape, size, sort

Algebra
- Recognize a qualitative property, or attribute
- Sort objects using a variety of attributes

Literacy

Oral Language Development
- Respond orally to simple questions
- Use mathematical terms

Comprehension
- Recall details
- Make connections using illustrations, prior knowledge, or real-life experiences
- Listen to a story being read aloud

Introducing the Concept

Begin the lesson by modeling how to sort red and blue crayons and markers into groups. Say:

I want to sort these crayons and markers. I want to put them into groups that are the same. I could sort them by color and put all of the red ones in this group and all of the blue ones in this group. I could sort them another way, too. I could sort them into a crayon group and a marker group.

Listening to the Story

Distribute the Day 1 activity page to each child. Say: *Listen and look at the picture as I read a story about a boy named Toby who is sorting buttons.*

Toby had a job to do. Toby's mom gave him a jar full of buttons. She asked him to sort the buttons into two groups. Toby carefully poured the buttons onto the table. He wondered how to sort them into groups. He looked carefully to see how the buttons were the same. He saw that some buttons had two holes and some had four holes. Toby sorted the buttons with two holes into one group. Then he put the buttons with four holes into another group. Soon, all the buttons had been sorted into two groups. "This job was easier than I thought," said Toby.

Confirming Understanding

Distribute crayons. Develop the math concept by asking children questions about the story. Ask:

- *What job did Toby do?* (sort buttons)
- *How did Toby sort the buttons?* (buttons with 2 holes/4 holes)
- *Look at the buttons on the table. Are they all the same size?* (no) *Are some buttons big?* (yes) *Are some buttons small?* (yes)
- *Now you draw 2 groups of buttons in the box below. Make 1 group of big buttons and 1 group of small buttons.*

Day 1 picture

Algebra

- Sort objects using a variety of attributes

Literacy

Oral Language Development

- Respond orally to simple questions
- Use number names

Comprehension

- Recall details

Reinforcing the Concept

Reread the Day 1 story. Then reinforce this week's math concept by discussing the story. Say:

In our story, Toby sorted the buttons into two groups. What two groups did he make? (buttons with 2 holes/buttons with 4 holes)

Distribute the Day 2 activity and crayons. Say:

- *Look at row 1. The first picture shows a shirt with buttons. Look at the other shirts in the row. Draw a circle around each shirt that has buttons. How many shirts did you circle?* (2)
- *Look at row 2. The first picture shows a shirt with no stripes. Look at the other shirts in the row. Draw a circle around each shirt with no stripes. How many shirts did you circle?* (2)
- *Look at row 3. The first picture shows a shirt with stripes. Look at the other shirts in the row. Draw a circle around each shirt with stripes. How many shirts did you circle?* (1)
- *Look at row 4. The first picture shows a shirt with short sleeves. Look at the other shirts in the row. Draw a circle around each shirt with short sleeves. How many shirts did you circle?* (1)

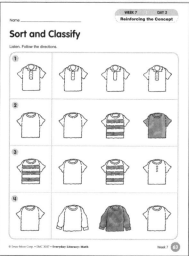

Name
WEEK 7 DAY 2
Reinforcing the Concept
Sort and Classify
Listen. Follow the directions.
1
2
3
4
Week 7 63

Day 2 activity

Day 3
SKILLS

Algebra

- Sort objects using a variety of attributes

Literacy

Oral Language Development

- Respond orally to simple questions

Comprehension

- Make connections using illustrations, prior knowledge, or real-life experiences

Applying the Concept

Introduce the activity by reviewing ways to sort:

You've learned that you can sort many things into groups. Look around the room. What things can we sort into groups? (big books/little books, toys with wheels/toys without wheels, etc.)

Distribute the Day 3 activity and crayons. Say:

- *This picture shows shoes. Let's find all the shoes with flowers. There are 3 of them. Color all the shoes with flowers red.*
- *Next, let's find all the shoes with laces. There are 3 of them. Circle all the shoes with laces.*
- *Now let's find all the shoes that you wear at the beach. There are 3 of them. Draw an* ***X*** *on all the shoes that you wear at the beach.*
- *Look at the shoes again. What are some other ways you could sort them?* (dark shoes/light shoes; shoes with dots/shoes without dots)

Name
WEEK 7 DAY 3
Applying the Concept
Sort and Classify
Listen. Sort the shoes.
64 Week 7

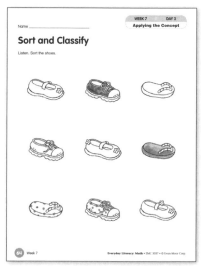

Day 3 activity

Algebra
• Sort objects using a variety of attributes

Number Sense
• Apply one-to-one correspondence while counting
• Understand that the final number counted in a set tells how many

Literacy

Oral Language Development
• Respond orally to simple questions
• Use number names

Comprehension
• Understand how mathematical ideas build on one another

Extending the Concept

Distribute the Day 4 activity and crayons. Then guide children through the activity by saying:

• *Let's sort these buttons into groups. Let's start by making a group of round buttons. Make a green dot on each round button.*

• *Next, find a square button. Make a blue dot on it. Make a blue dot on each square button.*

• *Now find a star-shaped button. Make a yellow dot on it. Make a yellow dot on the other star-shaped buttons.*

• *Finally, we'll make a group of heart-shaped buttons. Make a red dot on each heart-shaped button.*

• *Now we're going to count each type of button. First, count all of the round buttons that have a green dot on them. How many are there? (3) Look at the bottom of the page. Find the box that has a round button. Circle the 3 in this round button box.*

Repeat the process with the other button shapes.

Day 4 activity

Algebra
• Sort objects using a variety of attributes

Mathematical Thinking & Reasoning
• Use math to solve problems

Home–School Connection p. 66
Spanish version available (see p. 2)

Circle Time Math Activity

Reinforce this week's math concept with the following circle time activity:

Materials: children's shoes

Activity: Gather children in a circle and have them remove one shoe. Arrange the shoes in the center of the circle. Have children look at the shoes as you note their attributes. For example, say: *Some things about these shoes are different. Some things are the same. Some shoes are red. Some shoes have shoelaces. And some shoes have straps.*

Then ask children to sort the shoes. Help them decide on categories. For example, if sorting by color, have children choose a shoe to represent the brown group, a shoe for the red group, etc. Then invite children to take turns placing the remaining shoes in their corresponding groups.

After all of the shoes have been sorted, encourage children to say what they notice about the groups of shoes by modeling language. For example, say: *The group of brown shoes is big. The group of red shoes is small.*

Continue the activity by having children sort the shoes by other attributes.

© Evan-Moor Corp. • EMC 3037 • *Everyday Literacy: Math*

Name _____

Sort and Classify

Name _____

Sort and Classify

Listen. Follow the directions.

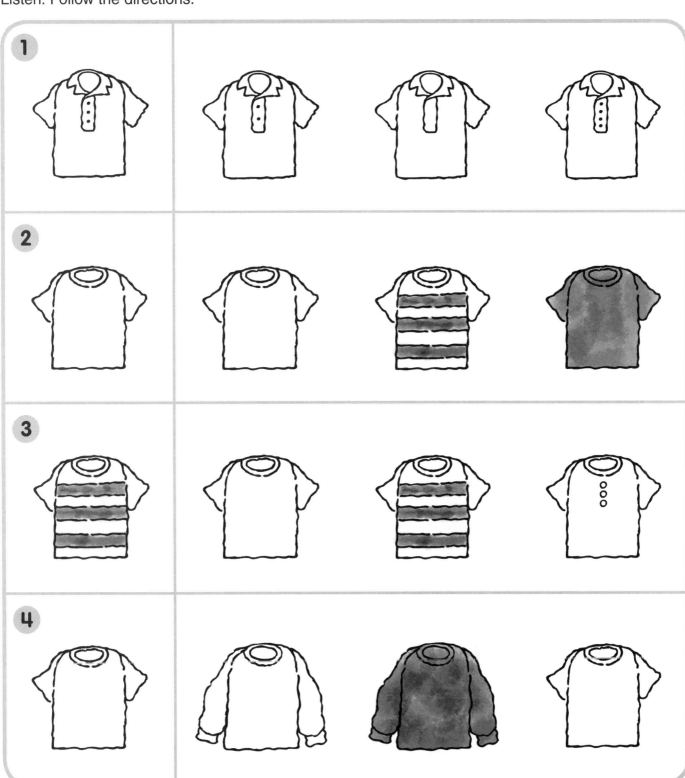

Name _____

Sort and Classify

Listen. Sort the shoes.

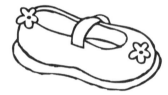

Name _____

Sort and Classify

Listen. Follow the directions.

1 2 3 4 5	1 2 3 4 5
1 2 3 4 5	1 2 3 4 5

Name _____

What I Learned

WEEK 7

Home–School Connection

Math Concept: Objects can be sorted into categories.

To Parents
This week your child learned how to sort and classify objects.

What to Do
Have your child look at the buttons below. Ask him or her to sort the buttons by shape. Have your child color the heart buttons red, the star buttons yellow, the square buttons blue, and the round buttons green.

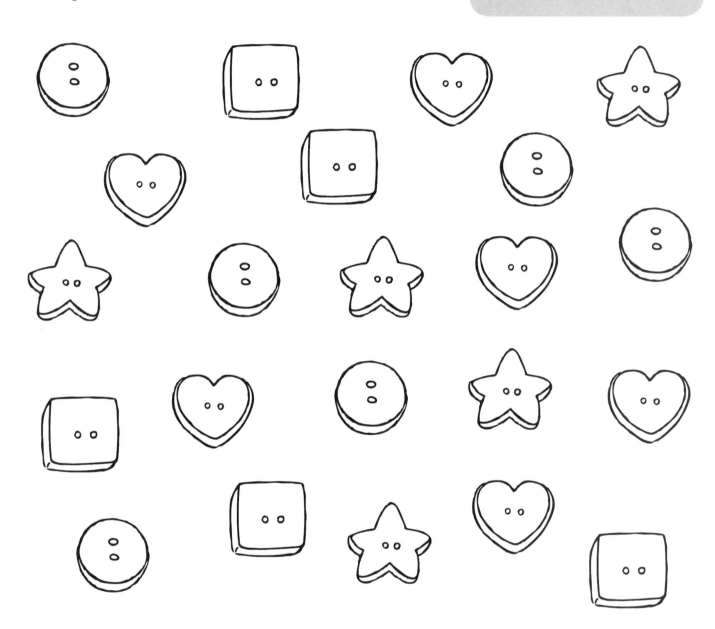

What to Do Next
Laundry day is a perfect time to practice sorting. Have your child sort clothing by color, by type of clothing item, or according to family member. After your child has sorted the laundry, have him or her explain the sorting system he or she used.

Everyday Literacy: Math • EMC 3037 • © Evan-Moor Corp.

Does It Belong?

Math Objective:

To help children discriminate like and unlike objects in a group

Math Vocabulary:

belong, same

Day 1
SKILLS

Algebra

• Discriminate like and unlike items

Literacy

Oral Language Development

• Respond orally to simple questions

• Use mathematical terms

Comprehension

• Recall details

• Make connections using illustrations, prior knowledge, or real-life experiences

• Listen to a story being read aloud

Introducing the Concept

Display two groups of items, such as crayons and wood blocks. Point out how each group contains items that are alike. Then hold up a red crayon and ask:

In which group does this red crayon belong? (in the crayon group)

Then add a crayon to the blocks group. Ask:

What item is <u>not</u> the same as the blocks? (crayon) *Why?* (All the other things in the group are blocks.) *That's right. The crayon does <u>not</u> belong in this group.*

Listening to the Story

Distribute the Day 1 activity page to each child. Say: *Listen and look at the picture as I read a story about a mom who finds an item that doesn't belong in her kitchen drawer.*

Today, Mom is making my favorite muffins. She has a special drawer for kitchen tools. The drawer has a mixing spoon, a whisk for beating eggs, and a spatula for mixing or stirring. When Mom reaches into the drawer to get the mixing spoon, she stops. "Hey!" she says. "Who left this hammer in my drawer?" Dad does not know how his hammer got in Mom's kitchen drawer. He takes his hammer and puts it where it belongs, with his other tools. But then Dad looks surprised. "Hey!" he says. "Who left this whisk in my toolbox?" It seems that today, things are <u>not</u> where they belong!

Confirming Understanding

Distribute crayons. Reinforce the math concept by asking questions about the story. Ask:

• *What belongs in Mom's kitchen drawer?* (mixing spoon, whisk, spatula) *What did Mom find in there that did <u>not</u> belong?* (hammer) *Draw an **X** on the hammer.*

• *Dad's hammer belongs in his toolbox, along with other tools for building and fixing. Does Mom's whisk belong in Dad's toolbox?* (no) *Why not?* (A whisk is not a building tool. It is used for beating eggs.) *Draw an **X** on the whisk.*

Day 1 picture

Algebra
• Discriminate like and unlike items

Literacy

Oral Language Development
• Respond orally to simple questions
• Use mathematical terms

Comprehension
• Recall details
• Make inferences and draw conclusions

Reinforcing the Concept

Reread the Day 1 story. Then reinforce this week's math concept by guiding a discussion about the story. Say:

Our story was about baking muffins. What did Mom find that did <u>not</u> belong? (a hammer)

Distribute the Day 2 activity and crayons. Say:

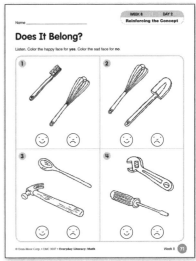

Day 2 activity

- *Point to box 1. The picture shows a toothbrush and a whisk. Do a toothbrush and a whisk belong together? Are they both baking tools? Color the happy face for **yes** or the sad face for **no**.* (no)

- *Point to box 2. The picture shows a whisk and a spatula. Do they belong together? Are they both baking tools? Color the happy face for **yes** or the sad face for **no**.* (yes)

- *Point to box 3. The picture shows a mixing spoon and a hammer. Do they belong together? Are they both baking tools? Color the happy face for **yes** or the sad face for **no**.* (no) *No, a hammer is not a baking tool.*

- *Point to box 4. The picture shows a wrench and a screwdriver. Do they belong together? Are they both building tools? Color the happy face for **yes** or the sad face for **no**.* (yes)

Algebra
• Discriminate like and unlike items

Literacy

Oral Language Development
• Respond orally to simple questions
• Use mathematical terms

Comprehension
• Make inferences and draw conclusions

Applying the Concept

Distribute the Day 3 activity and crayons. Then introduce the activity by saying:

Day 3 activity

- *Point to row 1. It shows a hammer, screwdriver, wrench, and ball. Three of these things belong together. The hammer, screwdriver, and wrench are tools. They belong together. Is a ball a tool?* (no) *The ball does <u>not</u> belong with the tools. Draw an **X** on the ball.*

- *Point to row 2. What do you see?* (fork, spoon, crayon, knife) *How are the fork, spoon, and knife the same?* (They are used for eating.) *Which item does <u>not</u> belong?* (crayon) *Why does the crayon not belong?* (The crayon is not used for eating. It is used for coloring.) *Draw an **X** on the crayon.*

- *Point to row 3. What do you see?* (stuffed monkey, teddy bear, toy car, stuffed elephant) *The monkey, teddy bear, and elephant are all toy animals. Which item does <u>not</u> belong?* (toy car) *Why does the toy car not belong?* (It is not an animal.) *Draw an **X** on the toy car.*

Algebra

- Discriminate like and unlike items

Literacy

Oral Language Development

- Respond orally to simple questions

Comprehension

- Make inferences and draw conclusions

Extending the Concept

Distribute the Day 4 activity and crayons. Then guide children through the activity by saying:

- *Point to box 1. What do you see?* (balls) *Which ball is different?* (small ball) *That's right. It doesn't belong. Why doesn't it belong?* (The other balls are big.) *Draw an X on the small ball.*

- *Point to box 2. What do you see?* (ice-cream cone, peanuts, milk, popcorn) *Which item doesn't belong?* (milk) *Why doesn't the milk belong?* (You can eat the other things, but you drink milk.) *Draw an X on the milk.*

- *Point to box 3. What do you see?* (marker, stapler, pencil, crayon) *Which item doesn't belong?* (stapler) *Why doesn't the stapler belong?* (You cannot write with it.) *Draw an X on the stapler.*

- *Point to box 4. What do you see?* (football, baseball, basketball, bat) *Which item doesn't belong?* (bat) *Why doesn't the bat belong?* (It is not a ball.) *Draw an X on the bat.*

Day 4 activity

Algebra

- Discriminate like and unlike items

Mathematical Thinking & Reasoning

- Use math to solve problems
- Explore mathematical ideas through song or play

Home–School Connection p. 74
Spanish version available (see p. 2)

Circle Time Math Activity

Reinforce this week's math concept with the following circle time activity:

Preparation: Have children form a circle.

Activity: Explain to children that they are going to play a game called "Does It Belong?" Think of a category. Point to and name three items that belong in that category and one that does not. For example, say:

I am going to name some furniture. One of the items <u>doesn't</u> belong. Tell me which one. Here we go:

Chair!

Table!

Bookshelf!

Flowers! (does <u>not</u> belong)

Continue with other categories that can be identified in the classroom, such as the following:

- Things to write with: pen/book*/pencil/crayon
- Clothing: dollhouse*/sweater/pants/jacket
- Toys: doll/teddy bear/clock*/ball

(*does not belong)

Name _____

Does It Belong?

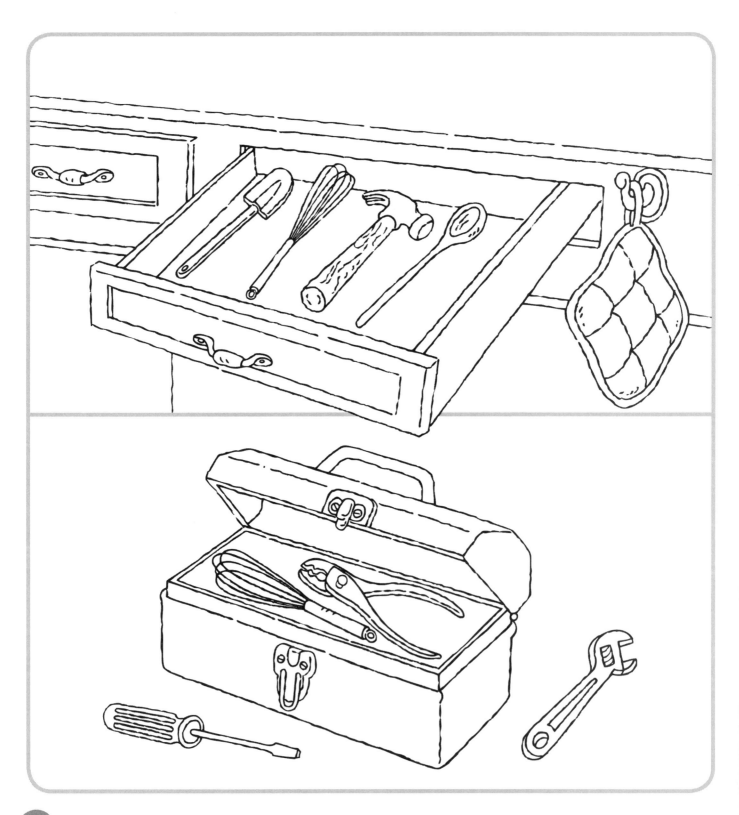

Everyday Literacy: Math • EMC 3037 • © Evan-Moor Corp.

Name _____

Does It Belong?

Listen. Color the happy face for **yes**. Color the sad face for **no**.

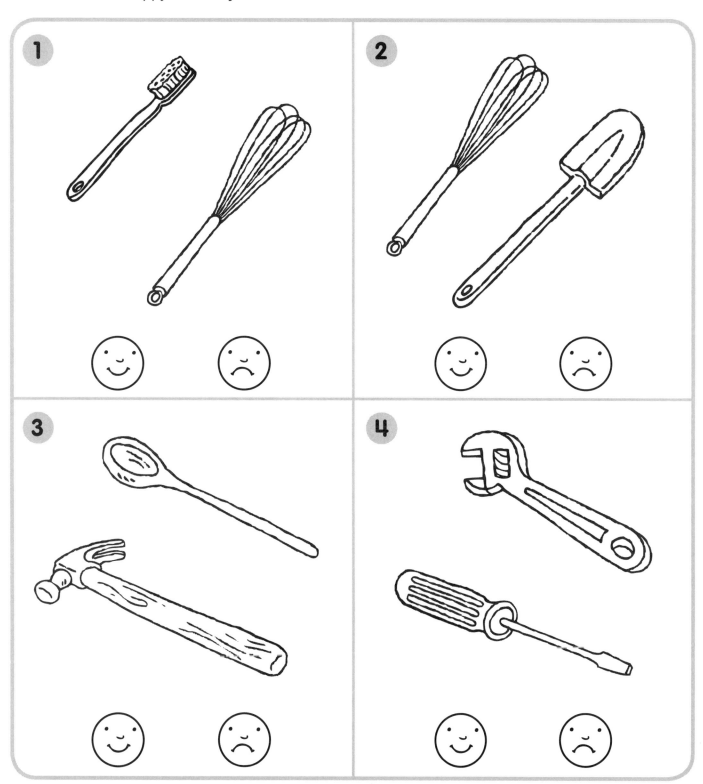

Name _____

Does It Belong?

Listen. Draw an **X** on the one that does <u>not</u> belong.

 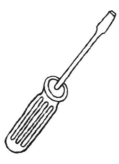  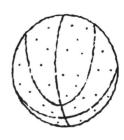

  Everyday Literacy: Math • EMC 3037 • © Evan-Moor Corp.

Name _____

Does It Belong?

Listen. Draw an **X** on the one that does <u>not</u> belong.

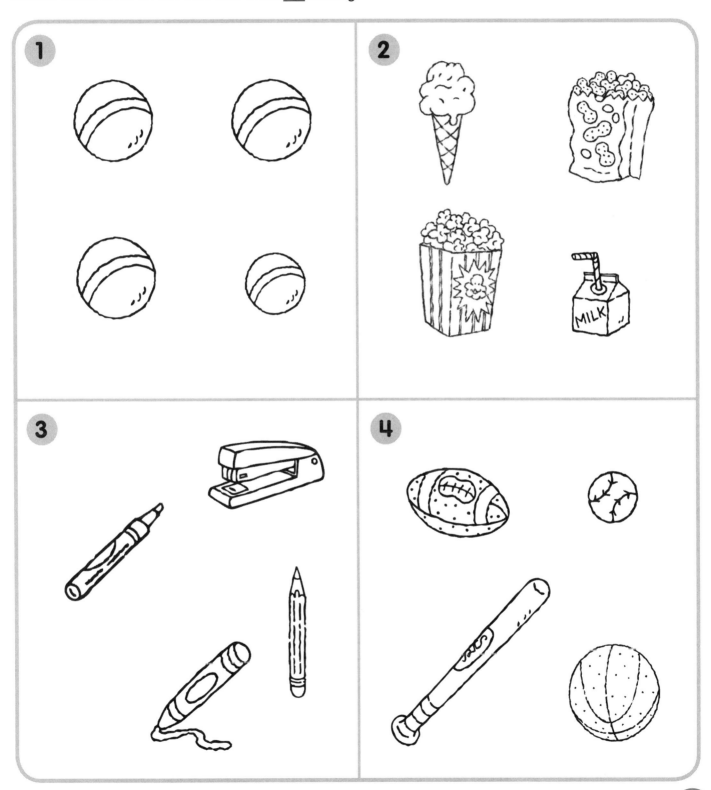

Name _____

What I Learned

What to Do
Have your child look at the picture below. Ask him or her to point to the item that does <u>not</u> belong in Mom's drawer, and then in Dad's drawer. Have him or her explain why. Then have your child color the picture.

Math Concept: Sets may have like and unlike items.

To Parents
This week your child learned how to find an item that does not belong in a group.

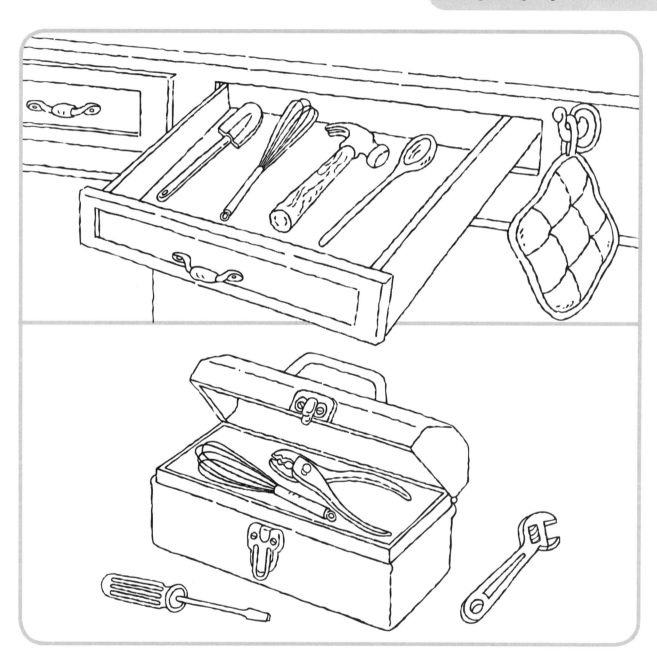

What to Do Next
Display sets of everyday items that belong together, such as a cup, plate, and saucer. Include an item that doesn't belong, such as an apple. Ask your child, *What doesn't belong?* (apple)

Concept

Certain words describe spatial relationships.

Where Is It?

Math Objective:

To help children describe spatial relationships of objects

Math Vocabulary:

down, in, next to, on, over, under, up

Day 1
SKILLS

Geometry

• Recognize and describe the spatial relationship between objects

Literacy

Oral Language Development

• Respond orally to simple questions

• Use mathematical terms

Comprehension

• Recall details

• Make connections using illustrations, prior knowledge, or real-life experiences

• Listen to a story being read aloud

Introducing the Concept

Before the lesson, place an object on a table, place another object under the table, and place a third object next to the table. Say:

*We can use words such as **in**, **on**, **under**, **up**, and **down** to tell where things are.*

- *Look at this table. What is **on** the table?* (children respond)
- *What is **under** the table?* (children respond)
- *What is **next to** the table?* (children respond)

Demonstrate **over** by holding an object over the table. Demonstrate **up** and **down** by raising an object up into the air and then lowering it to the table.

Listening to the Story

Distribute the Day 1 activity page. Say: *Listen and look at the picture as I read a story about children who go up and down and all around a playground.*

---

*Sam is swinging **on** a swing. Alex is going **up** the ladder, and Lily is zooming **down** the slide. Greta is **in** the sandbox. A ball is **next to** the sandbox. But Greta needs her shovel. Can you find it? There it is—**under** the slide!*

Confirming Understanding

Distribute crayons. Develop the math concept by asking questions about the story. Ask:

- *Is a child going **up** the ladder?* (yes) *Make a dot on that child.*
- *Circle the girl that is coming **down** the slide.*
- *What is flying **over** the swings?* (a bird) *Color the bird blue.*
- *What is **under** the slide?* (shovel) *Color the shovel red.*
- *What is **next to** the swings?* (a sandbox) *Make a yellow dot on the sand.*

Day 1 picture

Geometry

- Recognize and describe the spatial relationship between objects

Literacy

Oral Language Development

- Respond orally to simple questions
- Use mathematical terms

Comprehension

- Recall details
- Make connections using illustrations, prior knowledge, or real-life experiences

Reinforcing the Concept

Reread the Day 1 story. Then reinforce this week's math concept by guiding a discussion about the story. Say:

*Our story was about children who were playing. Words like **on, in, up, down,** and **under** tell where the children were. Where was Sam?* (on the swings) *Where was the bird?* (over the swings)

Distribute the Day 2 activity and crayons. Say:

- *Point to box 1. Is the bird **under** the tree? Color the happy face for **yes** or the sad face for **no**.* (no) *Where is the bird?* (**over** the tree)

- *Point to box 2. Is the ball **on** the table? Color the happy face for **yes** or the sad face for **no**.* (no) *Where is the ball?* (**under** the table)

- *Point to box 3. Is the shoe **next to** the ball? Color the happy face for **yes** or the sad face for **no**.* (yes)

- *Point to box 4. Is the boy **on** the bike? Color the happy face for **yes** or the sad face for **no**.* (no) *Where is the boy?* (**next to** the bike)

Day 2 activity

Geometry

- Recognize and describe the spatial relationship between objects

Literacy

Oral Language Development

- Respond orally to simple questions
- Use mathematical terms

Comprehension

- Make connections using illustrations, prior knowledge, or real-life experiences

Applying the Concept

To introduce the activity, describe where things are in your classroom. Say:

Words help us understand where things are.

- *What is **next to** the window?* (children respond)

- *What is **over** your head?* (children respond)

Distribute the Day 3 activity and crayons. Say:

- *Look at this picture. Point to the pond. What is swimming in the pond?* (a duck) *The duck is **in** the pond. Make a blue line **under** the duck.*

- *Point to the ball. Where is it?* (**under** the bench) *Draw another ball **on** the bench.*

- *Point to the tree. What is going **up** the tree?* (a squirrel) *Draw a purple line from the squirrel to the bird **on** the branch.*

- *Do you see a cat?* (yes) *What is the cat **next to**?* (the tree) *Make a green dot **over** the cat.*

Day 3 activity

Geometry

- Recognize and describe the spatial relationship between objects

Literacy

Oral Language Development

- Respond orally to simple questions
- Use mathematical terms
- Use number names

Comprehension

- Make connections using illustrations, prior knowledge, or real-life experiences

Applying the Concept

Distribute the Day 4 activity and crayons. Guide children through the activity by saying:

Day 4 activity

*Point to box 1. A little girl lost her shoes at the park. One shoe is **on** the swing.*

- *Where is the other shoe? (**under** the swing) Make a circle around the shoe that is **under** the swing.*

*Point to box 2. Two children are on the slide. One child is going **up** the ladder. With your finger, go up the ladder.*

- *Another child is going **down** the slide. With your finger, go down the slide.*

- *With your crayon, make a circle around the child that is going **up** the ladder.*

Point to box 3. How many balls do you see? (3)

- *One ball is going **over** the sandbox. Color that ball green.*

- *Another ball is **in** the sandbox. Color that ball red.*

- *Where is the other ball? (**next to** the sandbox) Color that ball blue.*

*Point to box 4. How many birds are **in** the nest? (2)*

- *How many birds are sitting **next to** the nest? (1)*

- *Make a yellow dot **under** the tree branch.*

Geometry

- Recognize and describe the spatial relationship between objects

Literacy

Oral Language Development

- Use mathematical terms

Mathematical Thinking & Reasoning

- Explore mathematical ideas through song or play

Home–School Connection p. 82
Spanish version available (see p. 2)

Hands-on Math Activity

Reinforce this week's math concept with the following hands-on activity:

Take children outside to play "Follow the Leader." For the first round, you will be the leader. Have children follow you and mimic your movements as you recite the following chant, incorporating this week's vocabulary words:

Let's all put our hands up, hands up, hands up.
Let's all put our hands up. Follow me!

Let's all go over a rock, over a rock, over a rock.
Let's all go over a rock. Follow me!

Let's all go under a tree, under a tree, under a tree.
Let's all go under a tree. Follow me!

Continue the chant using the positional words *next to, on, down,* etc.

Name _____

Where Is It?

Name _____

Where Is It?

Listen. Color the happy face for **yes**. Color the sad face for **no**.

Name _____

Where Is It?

Listen. Follow the directions.

Everyday Literacy: Math • EMC 3037 • © Evan-Moor Corp.

Name _____

Where Is It?

Listen. Follow the directions.

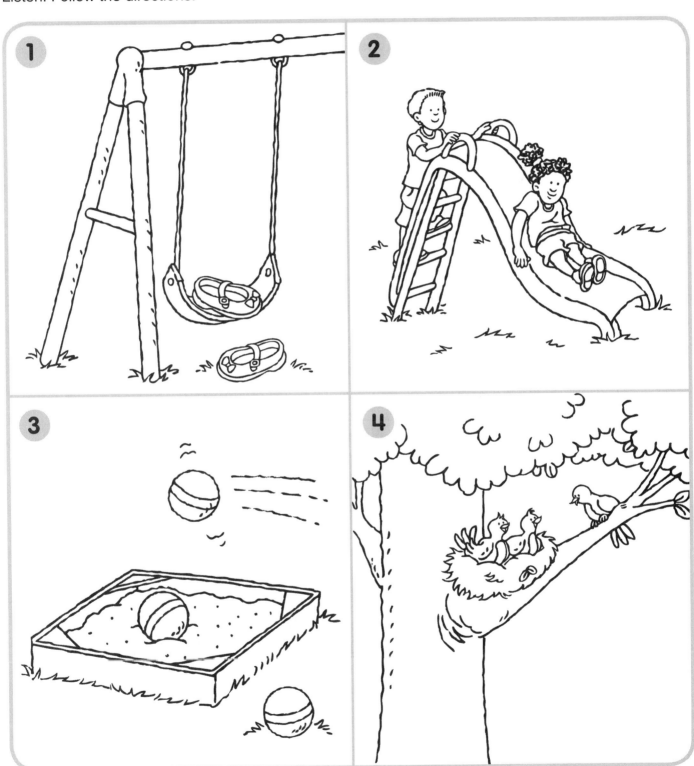

Name _____

What I Learned

What to Do

Have your child look at the picture and use words such as *on, in, up, down, next to, over,* and *under* to tell you what each child in the picture is doing and where he or she is. Then have your child color the picture.

Math Concept: Certain words describe spatial relationships.

To Parents
This week your child learned that we use certain words to tell where things and people are.

What to Do Next

Have your child play a game of "Where Is It?" Look around the room and ask questions about the location of objects, for example, *Where is the lamp?* (on the table)

Everyday Literacy: Math • EMC 3037 • © Evan-Moor Corp.

Time of Day

Math Objective:
To help children understand basic time concepts

Math Vocabulary:
after, afternoon, before, morning, night

Day 1
SKILLS

Measurement
• Understand basic time
concepts

Literacy

**Oral Language
Development**
• Respond orally to simple
questions
• Use vocabulary related
to time concepts

Comprehension
• Recall details
• Make connections
using illustrations, prior
knowledge, or real-life
experiences
• Listen to a story being
read aloud
• Make inferences and
draw conclusions

Introducing the Concept

Distribute the Day 1 activity page. Point to each row as you talk about it. Say:

• *Point to row 1. The picture shows the sun rising. There is a girl waking up in the morning. The sun rises at the beginning of the day. The beginning of the day is called the* **morning**. *You get dressed, eat breakfast, and brush your teeth in the morning.*

• *Point to row 2. The picture shows a girl playing in the afternoon. The* **afternoon** *is the middle of the day. You eat lunch, you play, and you nap.*

• *This bottom row shows the night.* **Night** *is the end of the day. It is dark outside. You get ready for bed and you brush your teeth. Show me or tell me what you do at night.* (put on pajamas; brush teeth)

Listening to the Story

Redirect children's attention to the Day 1 page. Say: *This girl is named Rosa. I will read a story about Rosa's day. Look at the pictures. Listen carefully.*

"Time to wake up, Rosa," said Rosa's dad. Rosa slid her legs out of bed and stretched her arms. Her cat Bosco stretched, too. Rosa got dressed and hurried into the kitchen. She ate cereal for breakfast. Then she went to school. In the afternoon, Rosa came home and ate pizza. After lunch, she and Bosco went outside to explore. It was a fun day! At night, Rosa was tired. She put on her pajamas and crawled into bed. She saw the moon and the stars and then she closed her eyes.

Confirming Understanding

Distribute crayons. Reinforce the math concept by talking about the story. Ask:

• *When does Rosa eat breakfast?* (morning) *Does the sun rise in the morning?* (yes) *Make a yellow dot on the sun.*

• *When do Rosa and her cat go exploring?* (afternoon) *Circle the cat.*

• *Which picture shows night?* (girl in bed) *How do you know it's night?* (The moon is in the sky; Rosa is in bed.) *Make a blue dot on the moon.*

Day 1 picture

Measurement

• Understand basic time concepts

Literacy

Oral Language Development

• Respond orally to simple questions

• Use vocabulary related to time concepts

Comprehension

• Recall details

• Make connections using illustrations, prior knowledge, or real-life experiences

Reinforcing the Concept

Reread the Day 1 story. Then reinforce this week's math concept by guiding a discussion about the story. Say:

Our story was about Rosa's day. What did Rosa do in the morning? (got dressed, ate breakfast) *In the afternoon?* (ate lunch and played outside) *At night?* (went to sleep)

Day 2 activity

Distribute the Day 2 activity and crayons. Say:

• *Point to box 1. At night, you might see stars in the sky. Does this picture show night? Color the happy face for **yes** or the sad face for **no**.* (no) *What is in the sky?* (sun)

• *Point to box 2. The sun rises, or comes up, in the morning. Does this picture show the sun rising? Color the happy face for **yes** or the sad face for **no**.* (yes)

• *Point to box 3. In the afternoon, Rosa ate pizza. Does this picture show what Rosa ate in the afternoon? Color the happy face for **yes** or the sad face for **no**.* (no) *What does it show?* (cereal) *When did she eat cereal?* (in the morning)

• *Point to box 4. In the morning, Rosa woke up and stretched. Does this picture show Rosa in the morning? Color the happy face for **yes** or the sad face for **no**.* (no) *What time of day is it?* (night)

Measurement

• Understand basic time concepts

Literacy

Oral Language Development

• Respond orally to simple questions

• Use vocabulary related to time concepts

Comprehension

• Make connections using illustrations, prior knowledge, or real-life experiences

• Make inferences and draw conclusions

Applying the Concept

To introduce the activity, guide a discussion that helps children recall the Day 1 story. Say:

*After lunch, Rosa and her cat went outside to explore. What do you do **before** lunch to get ready to eat?* (wash hands, set table, etc.) *What do you do **after** lunch when you finish eating?* (children respond)

Day 3 activity

Distribute the Day 3 activity and crayons. Say:

• *Point to picture 1. **Before** breakfast, the cereal bowl is empty. Which picture shows what happens **after** pouring the cereal?* (cereal is in the bowl, ready to eat) *Draw a line to that picture. Good morning!*

• *Point to picture 2. **Before** lunch, we wash our hands. Which picture shows what happens **after** we wash our hands?* (We eat lunch.) *Draw a line to that picture. Good afternoon!*

• *Point to picture 3. **Before** going to sleep, we put on pajamas. Which picture shows what happens **after** we put on pajamas?* (We go to sleep.) *Draw a line to that picture. Good night!*

Everyday Literacy: Math • EMC 3037 • © Evan-Moor Corp.

Day 4 SKILLS

Measurement

- Understand basic time concepts

Literacy

Oral Language Development

- Respond orally to simple questions
- Use vocabulary related to time concepts

Comprehension

- Make connections using illustrations, prior knowledge, or real-life experiences
- Make inferences and draw conclusions

Applying the Concept

Distribute the Day 4 activity and crayons. Then guide children through the activity by saying:

WEEK 10 DAY 4
Applying the Concept
Name
Time of Day
Listen. Circle what happened before.
1
2
3
4
© Evan-Moor Corp. • EMC 3037 • Everyday Literacy: Math
Week 10 69

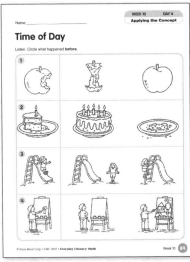

Day 4 activity

- *Look at row 1. This is an apple with a bite taken out. What do the other two pictures show?* (apple core; whole apple) *Which picture shows the apple* ***before*** *the bite was taken out?* (whole apple) *Make a circle around the picture of the whole apple.*
- *Look at row 2. What do you see?* (slice of cake) *What do the other two pictures show?* (whole cake and empty cake plate) *What did the cake look like* ***before*** *it had a slice cut from it?* (It was a whole cake.) *Make a circle around the picture of the whole cake.*
- *Look at row 3. Here is a girl going down the slide. What happened* ***before*** *she went down the slide?* (She went up the ladder.) *That's right. Make a circle around the picture of the girl going up the ladder.*
- *Look at row 4. Here is a boy painting a picture. What happened* ***before*** *he painted the picture?* (There was a blank paper.) *Make a circle around the picture of the boy with the blank paper.*

Day 5 SKILLS

Measurement

- Understand basic time concepts

Literacy

Oral Language Development

- Use vocabulary related to time concepts

Mathematical Thinking & Reasoning

- Explore mathematical ideas through song or play

Home-School Connection p. 90
Spanish version available (see p. 2)

Circle Time Math Activity

Reinforce this week's math concept with the following circle time activity:

Have children form a circle. Review the concept of morning, afternoon, and night with this song, sung to the tune of "Itsy Bitsy Spider":

Good morning, Mr. Sun, it's time to start my day.
(spread hands and arms like rays of sun)

All afternoon, I run around and play.
(run in place)

I go out and explore and I even ride a bike.
(pretend to ring bicycle bell: ding, ding!)

But now the fun is over.
It's time to say good night!
(lay head down on hands and sleep)

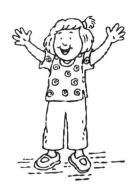

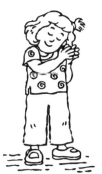

Name _____

Time of Day

Everyday Literacy: Math • EMC 3037 • © Evan-Moor Corp.

Name _____

Time of Day

Listen. Color the happy face for **yes**. Color the sad face for **no**.

Name _____

Time of Day

Listen. Draw lines to match.

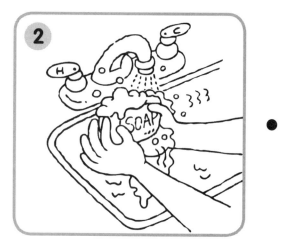

Everyday Literacy: Math • EMC 3037 • © Evan-Moor Corp.

Name _____

Time of Day

Listen. Circle what happened **before**.

Name _____

What I Learned

What to Do
Have your child look at the pictures below. Then have him or her identify **morning**, **afternoon**, and **night** and point out what happens at each time during Rosa's day. Next, compare Rosa's day to a typical day in your child's life.

Math Concept: Certain words describe time concepts.

To Parents
This week your child learned about the general sequence of time.

What to Do Next
Discuss today's events with your child. Prompt him or her by asking questions related to general sequence of time, such as, *What happened in the morning? What happened after that?*

Everyday Literacy: Math • EMC 3037 • © Evan-Moor Corp.

Concept

Counting tells how many objects are in a set.

Count to 10

Math Objective:

To help children count 10 or fewer objects in a set

Math Vocabulary

one, two, three, four, five, six, seven, eight, nine, ten, count, group, number

Day 1 SKILLS

Number Sense

• Apply one-to-one correspondence while counting

• Understand the relationship between numbers and quantities

• Recognize the symbols that represent numbers

• Associate each number with one name

Literacy

Oral Language Development

• Respond orally to simple questions

• Use number names

Comprehension

• Recall details

• Make connections using illustrations, prior knowledge, or real-life experiences

• Listen to a story being read aloud

Introducing the Concept

Before the lesson, identify objects in your classroom that can be part of a group that contains 10 or fewer objects, for example, letters, crayons, or name tags. Say:

Let's count some of the things in our room. How many tables are in the room? Let's count them together. (children respond)

Point to each object as you call out the number word together.

*We use numbers to count how many are in a group. Let's count how many fingers we have: **1, 2, 3, 4, 5, 6, 7, 8, 9, 10**.*

Continue pointing out different groups of objects until children are able to count varying quantities to 10.

Listening to the Story

Distribute the Day 1 activity page to each child. Say: *Listen and look at the picture as I read a story about a birthday boy who counts his gifts.*

---

*Today is Jack's birthday! He invited his friends to his party. Some of his friends are blowing bubbles outside. Three of his friends are inside with him, looking at the decorations. Colorful balloons make people happy. So do birthday gifts! Jack cannot wait to open his. He wonders how many gifts there are, so he counts: **1, 2, 3, 4, 5, 6**. Jack has six gifts so far!*

Confirming Understanding

Distribute crayons. Develop the math concept by asking children questions about the picture. Say:

• *Jack's mom decorated with balloons. How can we find out how many balloons there are?* (count) *Count the balloons.* (5) *Make a dot on each balloon as you count.*

• *How many of Jack's friends are inside?* (3) *Color each friend's party hat.*

• *Look at Jack's gifts on the table. How many gifts are there?* (6) *Draw an **X** on each gift as you count.*

Day 1 picture

Day 2 SKILLS

Number Sense

- Apply one-to-one correspondence while counting
- Understand the relationship between numbers and quantities
- Recognize the symbols that represent numbers
- Associate each number with one name

Literacy

Oral Language Development

- Respond orally to simple questions
- Use number names

Comprehension

- Recall details
- Make connections using illustrations, prior knowledge, or real-life experiences

Reinforcing the Concept

Reread the Day 1 story. Then reinforce this week's math concept by guiding a discussion about the story. Say:

Our story was about a boy named Jack. He received many gifts for his birthday. How many gifts were on the table? (6)

Distribute the Day 2 activity and crayons. Say:

Look at the picture. It's time to sing "Happy Birthday."

- *Point to the balloons. How can we find out how many balloons there are? (count) Count the balloons. Make a dot on each balloon as you count. (children count) How many did you count? (8)*

- *Point to Jack's cake. The candles tell how old Jack is. Let's count the candles together. Draw a line on each candle as you count: 1, 2, 3, 4. How old is Jack? (4)*

- *Some of the children left their cups on the table. How can we find out how many cups there are? (count) Yes, let's count the cups together. Draw an X on each cup as you count: 1, 2, 3, 4, 5. How many cups are there? (5)*

- *Do you see Jack's cats? They want to be at the party, too. How many cats do you see? (2) Draw a line under each cat as you count.*

Day 2 activity

Day 3 SKILLS

Number Sense

- Apply one-to-one correspondence while counting
- Understand the relationship between numbers and quantities
- Recognize the symbols that represent numbers
- Associate each number with one name

Literacy

Oral Language Development

- Respond orally to simple questions
- Use number names

Comprehension

- Recall details
- Make connections using illustrations, prior knowledge, or real-life experiences

Applying the Concept

To introduce the activity, remind children that numbers tell how many there is of something. Say:

Look around the room. How many windows are there? (children respond) How many tables are there? (children respond)

Distribute the Day 3 activity and crayons. Say:

- *Point to box 1. Does this picture show 6 balloons? Count to find out. Color the happy face for **yes** or the sad face for **no**. (no) How many balloons are there? (7)*

- *Point to box 2. Does this picture show 6 candles? Count to find out. Color the happy face for **yes** or the sad face for **no**. (yes)*

- *Point to box 3. Does this picture show 8 cups? Color the happy face for **yes** or the sad face for **no**. (no) How many cups are there? (9)*

- *Point to box 4. Does this picture show 10 forks? Color the happy face for **yes** or the sad face for **no**. (yes)*

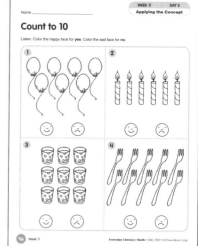

Day 3 activity

Number Sense

- Apply one-to-one correspondence while counting
- Understand the relationship between numbers and quantities
- Associate each number with one name

Literacy

Oral Language Development

- Respond orally to simple questions
- Use number names

Comprehension

- Make connections using illustrations, prior knowledge, or real-life experiences

Extending the Concept

Distribute the Day 4 activity and crayons. Introduce the activity by saying:

We use numbers to count. Let's count how many are in each of these groups.

- *Point to the balls. Count the balls.* (children count) *How many are there?* (5) *In the empty box next to the balls, draw **5** balls.*

After children finish drawing, say:

- *Count the balls you drew. Make sure there are **5**.*

- *Point to the cupcakes. Count the cupcakes.* (children count) *How many are there?* (4) *In the empty box next to the cupcakes, draw **4** cupcakes.*

After children finish drawing, say:

- *Count the cupcakes. Make sure you have **4**.*

- *Point to the flowers. Count the flowers.* (children count) *How many are there?* (6) *In the empty box next to the flowers, draw **6** flowers.*

After children finish drawing, say:

- *Count the flowers. Make sure you have **6**.*

Then have children color their drawings. Encourage them to count each item as they color it.

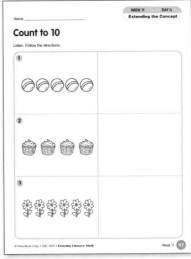

Day 4 activity

Number Sense

- Apply one-to-one correspondence while counting
- Understand the relationship between numbers and quantities

Literacy

Oral Language Development

- Use number names

Mathematical Thinking & Reasoning

- Explore mathematical ideas through song or play

Home–School Connection p. 98
Spanish version available (see p. 2)

Hands-on Math Activity

Reinforce this week's math concept with the following hands-on activity:

To practice counting to 10, have children play "Mother May I?" To begin, line children up in a horizontal line. Announce that you will be the mother. Stand about 20 feet away from children. Then choose a child to give a command to, following this pattern:

Mother: *Tyler, take five baby steps forward.*

Tyler: *Mother, may I?*

Mother: *Yes, you may.* (or *No, you may not.*)

Make sure each child requests permission before performing your command. Otherwise, say, *You did not say "Mother, may I?" You must stay where you are.* Encourage all the children to count aloud as the actions are being performed. The first child to tag Mother is the winner and becomes the next Mother (or Father).

Here are other commands to give children: *take one giant step forward; take seven baby steps backward; take four bunny hops forward;* etc.

Name _____

Count to 10

Name _____

Count to 10

Listen. Follow the directions.

Name _____

Count to 10

Listen. Color the happy face for **yes**. Color the sad face for **no**.

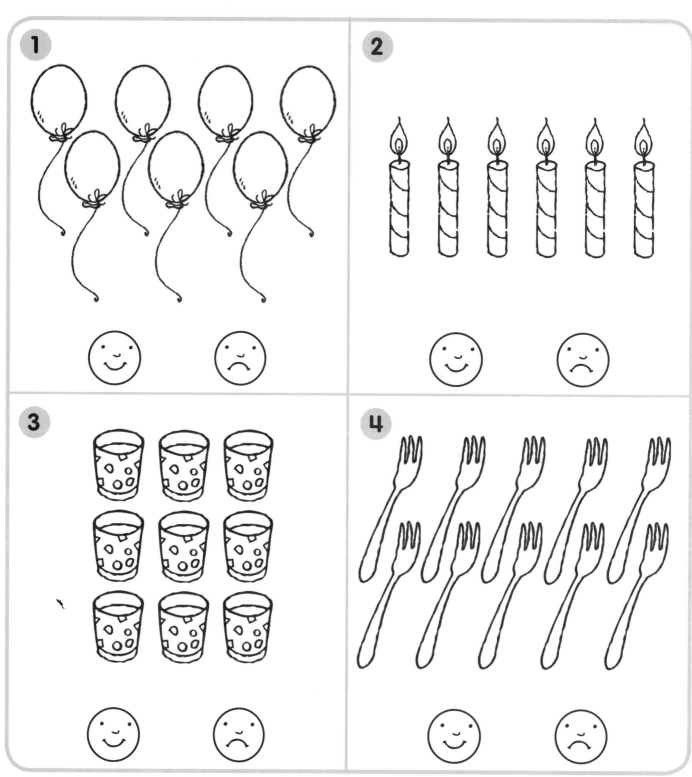

Everyday Literacy: Math • EMC 3037 • © Evan-Moor Corp.

Name _____

Count to 10

Listen. Follow the directions.

Name _____

What I Learned

What to Do

Look at the picture below with your child. Point out the different objects, such as balloons and cups, and ask your child to count how many of each object there is. Then have him or her color the picture.

WEEK 11

Home–School Connection

Math Concept: Counting tells how many objects are in a set.

To Parents

This week your child learned to count and produce 10 or fewer objects in a set.

What to Do Next

As you go about your daily routine, encourage your child to count objects up to 10. For example, as you set the table, ask: *How many plates are on the table? How many spoons?* Look for similar counting opportunities at the grocery store: *Hand me 3 cans of tomatoes, please. Now help me choose 6 oranges.*

What's the Number?

WEEK 12

Concept
Each number has a name and a symbol.

Math Objective:
To help children recognize and name numbers 1 through 10

Math Vocabulary:
one, two, three, four, five, six, seven, eight, nine, ten, number line

Day 1
SKILLS

Number Sense
- Understand the relationship between numbers and quantities
- Recognize the symbols that represent numbers
- Associate each number with one name

Literacy

Oral Language Development
- Respond orally to simple questions
- Use number names

Comprehension
- Make connections using illustrations, prior knowledge, or real-life experiences
- Listen to a story being read aloud

Introducing the Concept

Display a number line that begins with **1** and ends with **10**. Say:

This is a number line. It shows numbers 1 through 10. Name the numbers with me: 1, 2, 3, 4, 5, 6, 7, 8, 9, 10.

Next, have children identify numbers from 6 to 10 on the number line. Say:

Listen to the number I say. Point to it on the number line.

Then trace each number with your finger and have children use their fingers to form each number in the air.

Listening to the Story

Distribute the Day 1 activity page. Say: *Listen and look at the picture as I read about three children who are playing a game of cards with numbers.*

"Let's play! I will deal the cards," said Mae. She gave six cards to each player. Each card had a number. The number told how many pieces of fruit were on the card. Jake went first. He said, "Luke, do you have nine cherries?" Luke looked at all his cards. He saw a card that had a number 9 at the top, plus nine cherries. This was the card that Jake wanted, so Luke gave it to him. Now it was Jake's turn. He asked Mae if she had five pears. Mae did not have a card with the number 5 and five pears, so she said "no." Luke, Jake, and Mae had fun playing with the fruity number cards.

Confirming Understanding

Distribute crayons. Develop the math concept by asking children questions about the story. Ask:

- *What fruit is on card number 7?* (strawberries) *Point to the number 7. Now draw a red circle around the number 7.*

Repeat this process with numbers **6** and **9**. Then ask:

- *What number is on the card with the oranges?* (8) *Color the oranges orange.*

- *What number is on the card with the grapes?* (10) *Color the grapes green.*

Repeat this process with the cherries card and the apples card.

Day 1 picture

Number Sense

• Understand the relationship between numbers and quantities

• Recognize the symbols that represent numbers

• Associate each number with one name

Literacy

Oral Language Development

• Respond orally to simple questions

• Use number names

Comprehension

• Recall details

• Make connections using illustrations, prior knowledge, or real-life experiences

• Make inferences and draw conclusions

Reinforcing the Concept

Reread the Day 1 story. Then reinforce this week's math concept by guiding a discussion about the story. Say:

Our story was about a card game with numbers and fruit. What did the number on each card tell us? (how many pieces of fruit were on each card)

Distribute the Day 2 activity and crayons. Say:

• *Point to box 1. What fruit do you see?* (cherries) *How can we find out how many cherries there are?* (by counting) *Count the cherries.* (children count) *Are there 3, 4, or 5 cherries?* (5) *Circle the number 5.*

• *Point to box 2. What fruit do you see?* (strawberries) *How can we find out how many strawberries there are?* (by counting) *Count the strawberries.* (children count) *Are there 6, 7, or 8 strawberries?* (7) *Circle the number 7.*

• *Point to box 3. What fruit do you see?* (bananas) *Count the bananas.* (children count) *Are there 8, 9, or 10 bananas?* (10) *Circle the number 10.*

• *Point to box 4. What fruit do you see?* (apples) *Count the apples.* (children count) *Are there 4, 5, or 6 apples?* (6) *Circle the number 6.*

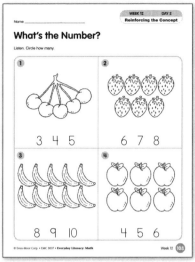

Day 2 activity

Number Sense

• Understand the relationship between numbers and quantities

• Recognize the symbols that represent numbers

• Associate each number with one name

Literacy

Oral Language Development

• Respond orally to simple questions

• Use number names

Comprehension

• Make connections using illustrations, prior knowledge, or real-life experiences

• Make inferences and draw conclusions

Applying the Concept

Distribute the Day 3 activity and crayons. Then introduce the activity by saying:

Each number has a name: 1, 2, 3, 4, 5, 6, 7, 8, 9, 10. We use numbers to tell how many.

• *Point to the cherries. How many cherries are there?* (10) *Draw a line from the cherries to the number 10. Now trace the number 10.*

• *Point to the strawberries. How many strawberries are there?* (9) *Draw a line from the strawberries to the number 9. Now trace the number 9.*

• *Point to the pears. How many pears are there?* (6) *Draw a line from the pears to the number 6. Now trace the number 6.*

• *Point to the lemons. How many lemons are there?* (8) *Draw a line from the lemons to the number 8. Now trace the number 8.*

• *Point to the bananas. How many bananas are there?* (7) *Draw a line from the bananas to the number 7. Now trace the number 7.*

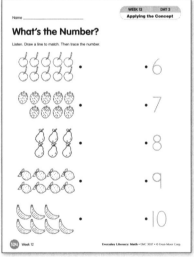

Day 3 activity

Extending the Concept

Distribute the Day 4 activity and crayons. Then introduce the activity by saying:

There is a picture hiding here. You will use your crayons to color. I will tell you what color to use for each number. Listen carefully.

- *Find all the spaces that have the number **6** on them. Color those spaces red. There are four spaces with the number **6**. Make sure you color them all.*

- *Now find all the spaces with the number **7**. Color those spaces yellow. There are three spaces with the number **7**.*

- *Now find all the spaces with the number **8**. Color those spaces purple.*

- *Now find all the spaces with the number **9**. Color those spaces green.*

- *Now find the one space that has the number **10** on it. Color this space orange.*

- *What do you see?* (apple, pear, banana, orange, grapes)

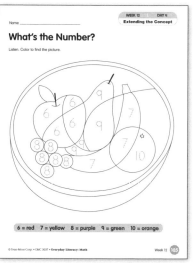

Day 4 activity

Circle Time Math Activity

Reinforce this week's math concept with the following circle time activity:

Materials: 10 sheets of sturdy paper, markers, Day 1 activity page

Preparation: On each sheet of paper, draw each fruity number card from Day 1.

Activity: Display the cards in order from **10** to **1**. Review the number name and the fruit name in random order: 10 grapes, 5 pears, etc.

Gather children in a circle. Teach them the following song called "The Ten Days of Preschool" (to the tune of "The Twelve Days of Christmas"). Point to each card as you mention it:

On the ten days of preschool my teacher gave to me:

Ten green grapes, nine little cherries, eight orange oranges, seven red strawberries, six crispy apples, five golden pears...

four ripe bananas, three sour lemons, two sweet pineapples, and one juicy watermelon!

After children are familiar with the song, distribute the cards randomly to children. Sing the song again, this time having the children listen for their fruit to be mentioned in the song and then raise their corresponding card.

Name _____

What's the Number?

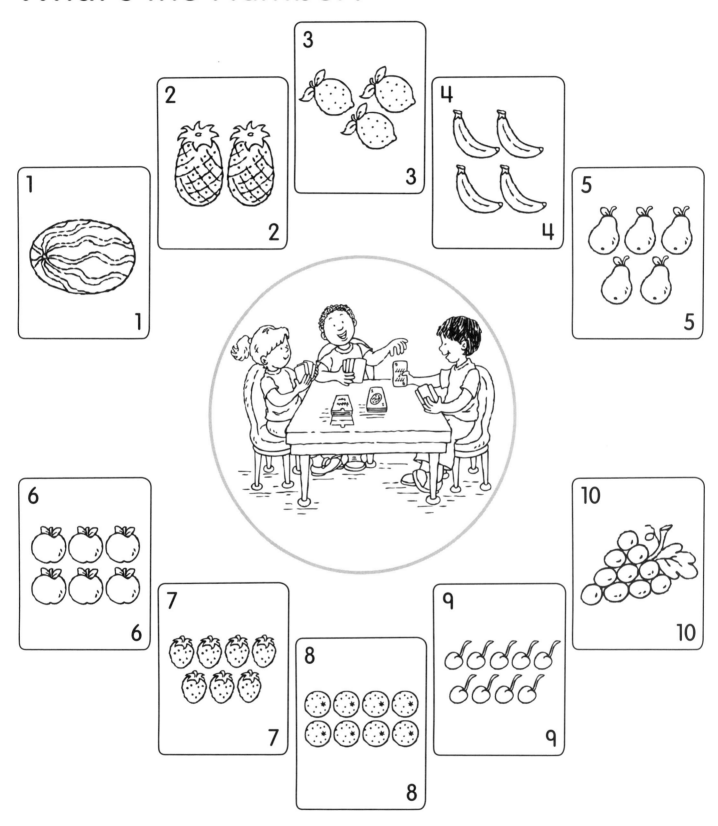

Everyday Literacy: Math • EMC 3037 • © Evan-Moor Corp.

Name _____

What's the Number?

Listen. Circle how many.

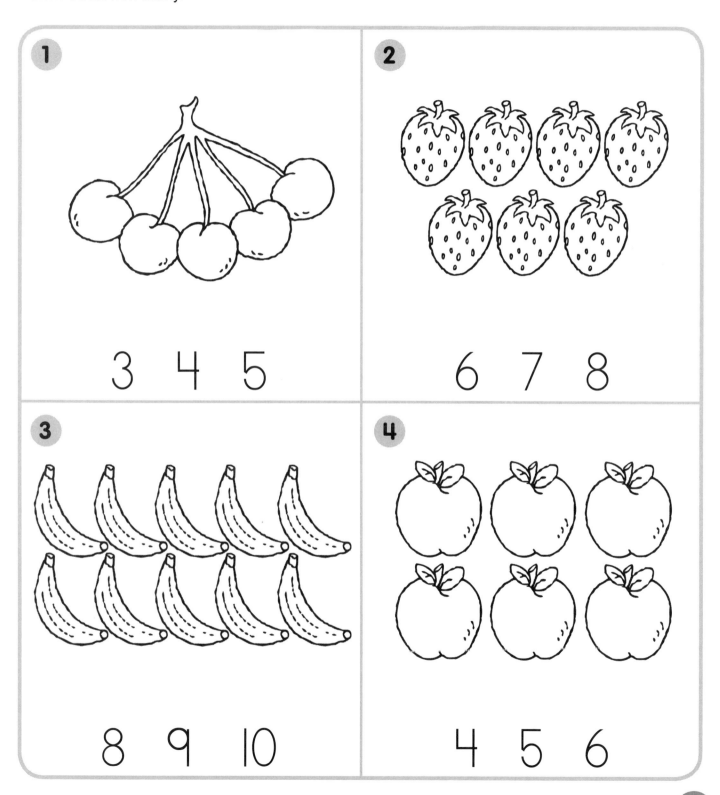

Name _____

What's the Number?

Listen. Draw a line to match. Then trace the number.

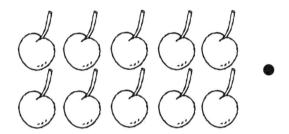   •   • 6

   •   • 7

   •   • 8

   •   • 9

   •   • 10

Name _____

What's the Number?

Listen. Color to find the picture.

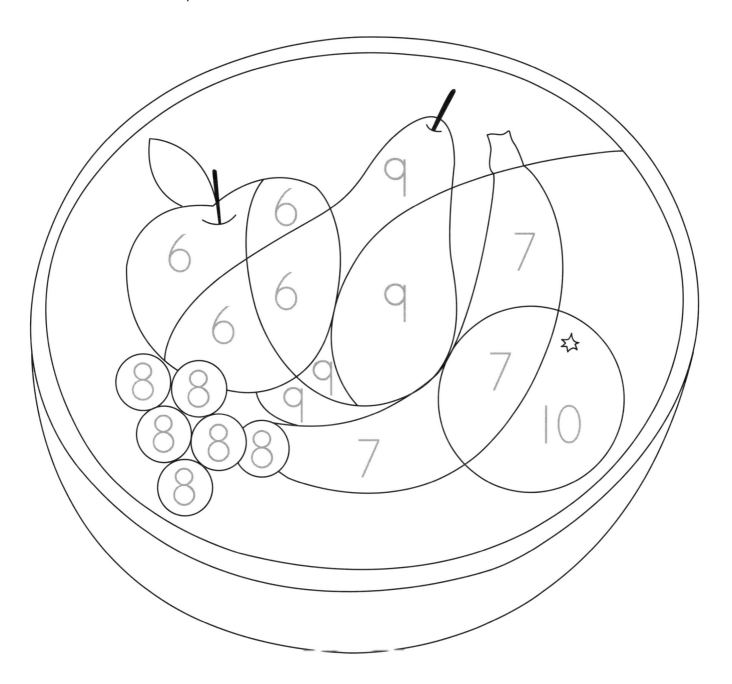

6 = red   7 = yellow   8 = purple   9 = green   10 = orange

Name _____

What I Learned

What to Do
Have your child look at the cards below. Ask your child to point to and name the numbers on the cards. Then have him or her color the fruit on the cards.

WEEK 12

Home–School Connection

Math Concept: Each number has a name and a symbol.

To Parents
This week your child learned to recognize, name, and form the numbers 1 through 10.

What to Do Next
To practice number recognition, play "Go Fish" with a deck of cards. Remove the jack, queen, king, and ace. Each player gets five cards. You go first. Ask for a card by number, for example, *Do you have any 5s?* You must be holding the card you are requesting. Your child must give you all the 5s he or she is holding. If your child does not have any 5s, he or she says, *Go Fish,* and you draw a card from the pile. The winner is the player who has the most pairs of same-number cards.

Everyday Literacy: Math • EMC 3037 • © Evan-Moor Corp.

More or Less

Math Objective:

To help children do mathematical comparisons

Math Vocabulary:

group, less, more, same

Day 1
SKILLS

Number Sense

• Match objects from two groups using one-to-one correspondence

• Compare relationships between quantities

Literacy

Oral Language Development

• Respond orally to simple questions

• Use mathematical terms

Comprehension

• Recall details

• Make connections using illustrations, prior knowledge, or real-life experiences

• Listen to a story being read aloud

Introducing the Concept

Begin the lesson by reviewing one-to-one correspondence. Construct a tower of 5 red blocks, having children count each block aloud as you place it. Next to it, construct a tower of 5 blue blocks, also counting each block. Ask:

*How many blocks does the red tower have? (5) How many blocks does the blue tower have? (5) Each tower has 5 blocks, so they have the **same** number of blocks.*

Add 2 more blocks to the red tower. Say:

*Look at the towers now. They are not the same anymore. They look different. The red tower has **more** blocks. The blue tower has **less**.*

Continue changing the quantity of blocks, asking, *Which has **more**? Which has **less**?*

Listening to the Story

Distribute the Day 1 activity page. Say: *Listen and look at the picture as I read a story about two children at a carnival.*

---

*Rey and Maria had fun at the school carnival. They played games and they won prizes. Both of them won goldfish. Rey won 3 goldfish. Maria also won 3 goldfish. They won the **same** number of goldfish. Rey and Maria won balloons. Rey won 2 balloons. Maria won 4 balloons. Maria won **more** balloons than Rey. Playing all these games was making Rey hungry. He said, "Let's go do the cakewalk and see if we can each win 1 cake!"*

Confirming Understanding

Distribute crayons. Develop the math concept by asking children questions about the picture. Say:

• *Look at the bowls of fish. Does Rey have **more** fish, **less** fish, or the **same** number of fish as Maria? (same) Draw a line from Rey's fishbowl to Maria's fishbowl.*

• *Look at the balloons. Who has **less** balloons? (Rey) Color Rey's balloons.*

• *Who has **more** balloons? (Maria) Draw an **X** on Maria's balloons.*

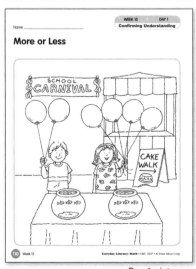

Day 1 picture

Number Sense

• Match objects from two groups using one-to-one correspondence

• Compare relationships between quantities

Literacy

Oral Language Development

• Respond orally to simple questions

• Use mathematical terms

Comprehension

• Recall details

• Make connections using illustrations, prior knowledge, or real-life experiences

Reinforcing the Concept

Reread the Day 1 story. Then reinforce this week's math concept by discussing the story. Say:

*Our story was about two children who each had 3 goldfish. Did Rey have the **same** number of goldfish as Maria?* (yes)

Distribute the Day 2 activity and crayons. Say:

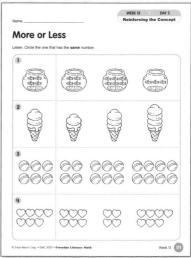

Day 2 activity

• *Point to row 1. The first picture shows **4** goldfish in a bowl. Look at the other bowls of goldfish. Circle the one that has the **same** number of goldfish as the first bowl.*

• *Point to row 2. The first picture shows an ice-cream cone with **3** scoops. Look at the other ice-cream cones. Circle the one that has the **same** number of scoops as the first cone.*

• *Point to row 3. The first picture shows **6** balls. Look at the other groups of balls. Circle the group that has the **same** number of balls as the first group.*

• *Point to row 4. The first picture shows **7** hearts. Look at the other groups of hearts. Circle the group that has the **same** number of hearts as the first group.*

Number Sense

• Match objects from two groups using one-to-one correspondence

• Compare relationships between quantities

Literacy

Oral Language Development

• Respond orally to simple questions

• Use mathematical terms

Comprehension

• Recall details

• Make connections using illustrations, prior knowledge, or real-life experiences

Applying the Concept

Distribute the Day 3 activity and crayons. Then guide children through the activity by saying:

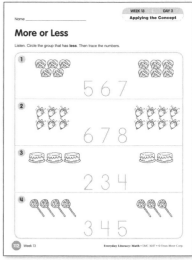

Day 3 activity

• *Look at row 1. There are two groups of pretzels. Circle the group that has **less** pretzels.* (children respond) *How many pretzels are in the group with less?* (5) *Trace the number **5**.*

• *Look at row 2. There are two groups of tops. Circle the group that has **less** tops.* (children respond) *How many tops are in the group with less?* (6) *Trace the number **6**.*

• *Look at row 3. There are two groups of cakes. Circle the group that has **less** cakes.* (children respond) *How many cakes are in the group with less?* (2) *Trace the number **2**.*

• *Look at row 4. There are two groups of lollipops. Circle the group that has **less** lollipops.* (children respond) *How many lollipops are in the group with less?* (3) *Trace the number **3**.*

Everyday Literacy: Math • EMC 3037 • © Evan-Moor Corp.

Day 4
SKILLS

Number Sense

• Match objects from two groups using one-to-one correspondence

• Compare relationships between quantities

Literacy

Oral Language Development

• Respond orally to simple questions

• Use mathematical terms

Comprehension

• Recall details

• Make connections using illustrations, prior knowledge, or real-life experiences

Extending the Concept

Distribute the Day 4 activity and crayons. Then guide children through the activity by saying:

> • *Look at row 1. There are two groups of stars. Count the stars in group 1.* (children count) *How many stars are there?* (4) *Trace the 4 under this group. Point to the next group of stars. Count the stars.* (children count) *How many stars are there?* (3) *Trace the 3 under this group. Now circle the group that has* **more** *stars.*

> • *Look at row 2. Here are two groups of flowers. Count the flowers in group 1.* (children count) *How many flowers are there?* (6) *Trace the 6 under this group. Point to the next group of flowers. Count the flowers.* (children count) *How many flowers are there?* (7) *Trace the 7 under this group. Now circle the group that has* **more** *flowers.*

> • *Look at row 3. There are two groups of candies. Count the candies in group 1.* (children count) *How many candies are there?* (9) *Trace the 9 under this group. Point to the next group of candies. Count the candies.* (children count) *How many candies are there?* (8) *Trace the 8 under this group. Now circle the group that has* **more** *candies.*

Day 4 activity

Day 5
SKILLS

Number Sense

• Compare relationships between quantities

Literacy

Oral Language Development

• Use mathematical terms

Mathematical Thinking & Reasoning

• Explore mathematical ideas through song or play

Home–School Connection p. 114
Spanish version available (see p. 2)

Hands-on Math Activity

Reinforce this week's math concept with the following hands-on activity:

Materials: sidewalk chalk; beanbags of various colors, 3 per small group

Preparation: Take children to an open area to play a beanbag-toss game. Divide children into small groups. On the pavement, draw one large circle for each group.

Activity: Have each group stand about five feet from a circle. Give three beanbags to the first player in each group. Have children take turns tossing the beanbags into the circle. Some may land inside the circle and some will land outside the circle. When children have finished tossing all their beanbags, have them stand back and survey the results. Ask questions such as,

> • *Are there* **more** *red beanbags or* **more** *blue beanbags inside the circle?*

> • *Are there the* **same** *number of green beanbags as blue beanbags?*

Name _____

More or Less

Name _____

More or Less

Listen. Circle the one that has the **same** number.

1

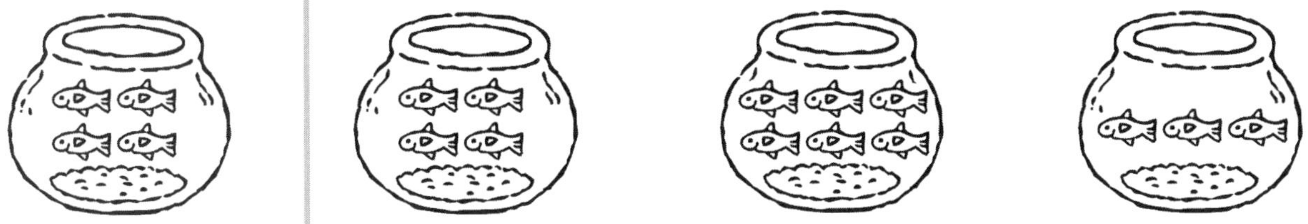

2

3

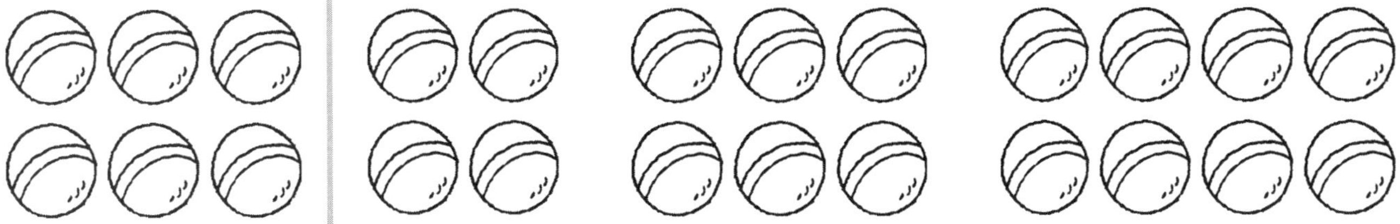

4

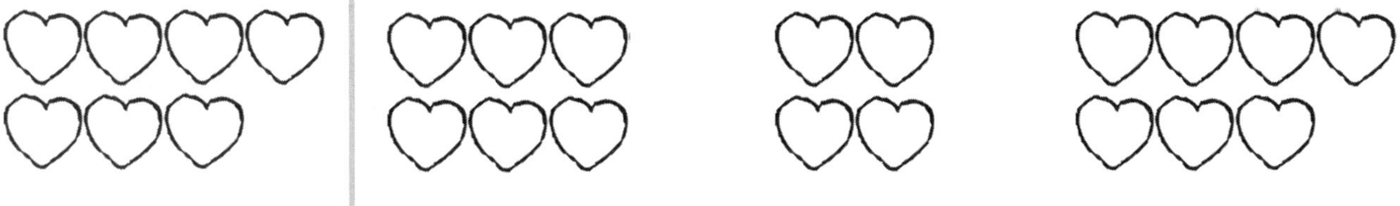

Name _____

More or Less

Listen. Circle the group that has **less**. Then trace the number.

1

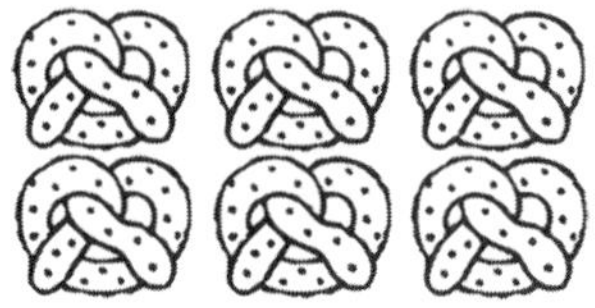

5 6 7

2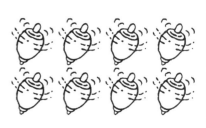

6 7 8

3

2 3 4

4

3 4 5

Name _____

More or Less

Listen. Count and trace. Circle the group that has **more**.

1

3 4 5    3 4 5

2

5 6 7    5 6 7

3

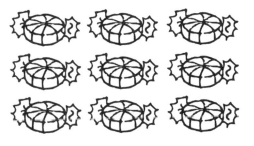

8 9 10 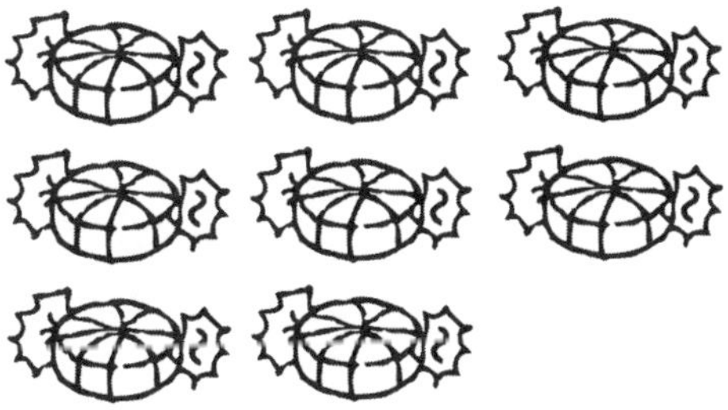   8 9 10

Name _____

What I Learned

What to Do
Have your child look at the picture below. It shows two children, Rey and Maria, at a carnival. Have your child tell you who has **more** balloons and who has **less** balloons. Then have him or her tell you if the children have **more**, **less**, or the **same** number of goldfish.

Math Concept: Use *more, less,* and *same* to compare quantities.

To Parents
This week your child learned to compare quantities using the words *more, less,* and *same.*

What to Do Next
Take a walk with your child. Along the way, have your child compare quantities in the environment by asking him or her questions such as, *Which yard has **more** trees, this one or that one?*

Concept

Addition is the operation of *adding to.*

One More

Math Objective:

To help children understand the meaning of the operation of addition

Math Vocabulary:

add, count, group, one more

Day 1
SKILLS

Number Sense

- Show an understanding of the quantity of one
- Understand that the final number counted in a set tells how many
- Understand that addition is *adding to*

Literacy

Oral Language Development

- Respond orally to simple questions
- Use number names

Comprehension

- Make connections using illustrations, prior knowledge, or real-life experiences
- Listen to a story being read aloud

Introducing the Concept

Use three blocks to model addition. Place two blocks on a table and say:

We can use numbers to show **one more***. Look at the blocks on the table. Count them with me: **1, 2**. I will add **one more** block. Now let's count the blocks: **1, 2, 3**. Two blocks and **one more** block are how many blocks?* (3 blocks)

Continue the process by adding one more block to three, four, and then five blocks.

Listening to the Story

Distribute the Day 1 activity page. Say: *I will read a poem about groups of crabs. Listen as **one more** crab comes to each group.*

One little crab
With nothing to do.
One more comes.
Then there are two.

Two little crabs
Swimming in the sea.
One more comes.
Then there are three.

Three little crabs
Walking on the shore.
One more comes.
Then there are four.

Four little crabs
Ready to dive.
One more comes.
Then there are five.

Confirming Understanding

Distribute crayons. Develop the math concept by asking questions about the poem. Say:

- *Point to the one little crab with nothing to do. Circle it with red.* **One more** *crab comes along. How can we find out how many crabs there are now?* (count) *Count the crabs.* (2)

- *Point to the two little crabs swimming in the sea. Circle them with blue.* **One more** *crab comes to swim. Count the crabs.* (3)

Repeat the process with three and four crabs.

Day 1 picture

Number Sense

- Show an understanding of the quantity of one
- Understand that the final number counted in a set tells how many
- Understand that addition is *adding to*

Literacy

Oral Language Development

- Respond orally to simple questions
- Use number names

Comprehension

- Recall details
- Make connections using illustrations, prior knowledge, or real-life experiences

Reinforcing the Concept

Reread the Day 1 story. Then reinforce this week's math concept by guiding a discussion about the poem. Say:

Our poem was about groups of crabs. How many crabs came along to join each group? (one more crab)

Distribute the Day 2 activity and crayons. Say:

- *Point to box 1. How many fish do you see?* (1) *Draw* **one more** *fish. How many fish are there now?* (2) *Circle the number* **2**.

- *Point to box 2. How many fish do you see?* (2) *Draw* **one more** *fish. How many fish are there now?* (3) *Circle the number* **3**.

- *Point to box 3. How many fish do you see?* (3) *Draw* **one more** *fish. How many fish are there now?* (4) *Circle the number* **4**.

- *Point to box 4. How many fish do you see?* (4) *Draw* **one more** *fish. How many fish are there now?* (5) *Circle the number* **5**.

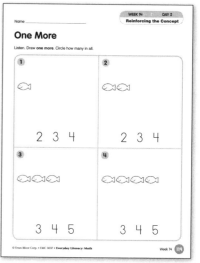

Day 2 activity

Number Sense

- Show an understanding of the quantity of one
- Understand that the final number counted in a set tells how many
- Understand that addition is *adding to*

Literacy

Oral Language Development

- Respond orally to simple questions
- Use number names

Comprehension

- Recall details
- Make connections using illustrations, prior knowledge, or real-life experiences

Applying the Concept

Distribute the Day 3 activity and crayons. Then introduce the activity by saying:

Our poem was about groups of crabs. Each group got one more crab. Here are groups of sea animals that will also get **one more** *each.*

- *Point to the sea stars in the box. How many sea stars are there?* (6) *Point to the sea star outside the box. Let's* **add** *it to the group. How many sea stars do we have now?* (7) *Draw a line to the* **7**. *Trace the* **7**. *Color all the sea stars orange.*

- *Point to the crabs. How many crabs are in the box?* (4) *Let's add* **one more**. *How many crabs do we have now?* (5) *Draw a line to the* **5**. *Trace the* **5**. *Color all the crabs blue.*

- *Point to the jellyfish. How many jellyfish are in the box?* (3) *Let's add* **one more**. *How many jellyfish do we have now?* (4) *Draw a line to the* **4**. *Trace the* **4**. *Color all the jellyfish yellow.*

- *Point to the seashells. How many seashells are in the box?* (7) *Let's add* **one more**. *How many seashells do we have now?* (8) *Draw a line to the* **8**. *Trace the* **8**. *Color all the seashells purple.*

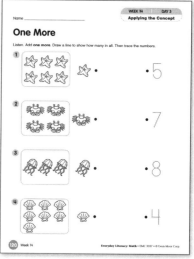

Day 3 activity

Number Sense

- Show an understanding of the quantity of one

- Understand that the final number counted in a set tells how many

- Understand that addition is *adding to*

Literacy

Oral Language Development

- Respond orally to simple questions

- Use number names

Comprehension

- Recall details

- Make connections using illustrations, prior knowledge, or real-life experiences

Applying the Concept

Distribute the Day 4 activity and crayons. Guide children through the activity by saying:

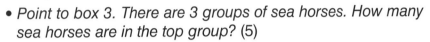

- *Point to box 1. There are 3 groups of whales. How many whales are in the top group?* (2)

- *Look at the other 2 groups of whales. Circle the group that has **one more** whale than the top group. How many are in the group that has one more whale?* (3)

- *Point to box 2. There are 3 groups of turtles. How many turtles are in the top group?* (4)

- *Look at the other 2 groups of turtles. Circle the group that has **one more** turtle. How many turtles are in the group that has one more?* (5)

- *Point to box 3. There are 3 groups of sea horses. How many sea horses are in the top group?* (5)

- *Circle the group that has **one more** sea horse. How many sea horses are in the group that has one more?* (6)

- *Point to box 4. There are 3 groups of crabs. How many crabs are in the top group?* (6)

- *Circle the group that has **one more** crab. How many crabs are in the group that has one more?* (7)

Day 4 activity

Number Sense

- Understand that the final number counted in a set tells how many

- Understand that addition is *adding to*

Literacy

Oral Language Development

- Use number names

Mathematical Thinking & Reasoning

- Explore mathematical ideas through song or play

Home–School Connection p. 122

Spanish version available (see p. 2)

Circle Time Math Activity

Reinforce this week's math concept with the following circle time activity:

Preparation: Teach children the song below to the tune of "Five Little Ducks."

Activity: Have children form a circle. Explain that they will hold hands and swing their arms back and forth to represent ocean waves as they sing. Have one child stand in the middle of the circle, wiggling and swimming like a little fish.

One little fish went out to play.

Deep in the ocean far away.

He was having so much fun,

*He called for **one more** fish to come.*

(One more child joins the first one in the center.)

Two little fish went out to play.

Deep in the ocean far away.

They were having so much fun,

*They called for **one more** fish to come.*

(One more child joins the two in the center, and so on.)

Continue singing until 10 children are in the center. Then start over.

Name _____

One More

Everyday Literacy: Math • EMC 3037 • © Evan-Moor Corp.

Name ______________________________

One More

Listen. Draw **one more**. Circle how many in all.

1

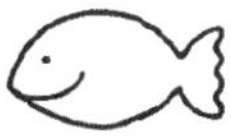

2 3 4

2

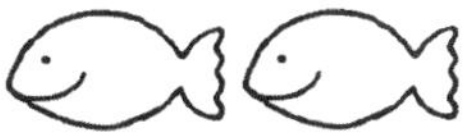

2 3 4

3

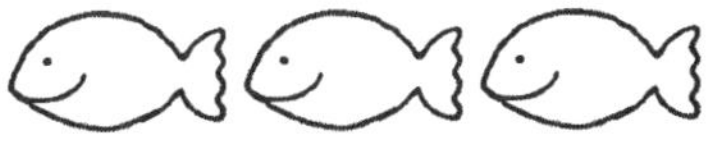

3 4 5

4

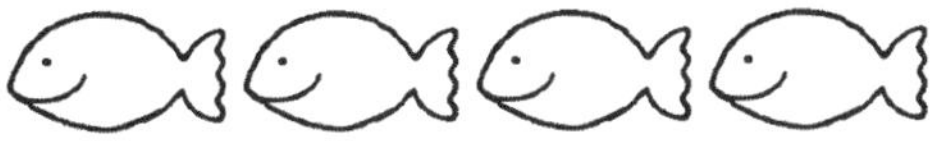

3 4 5

Name _____

One More

Listen. Add **one more**. Draw a line to show how many in all. Then trace the number.

1  • •5

2 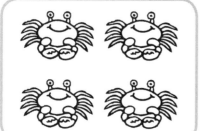  • •7

3  • •8

4  • •4

Everyday Literacy: Math • EMC 3037 • © Evan-Moor Corp.

Name _____

One More

Listen. Circle the group that has **one more**.

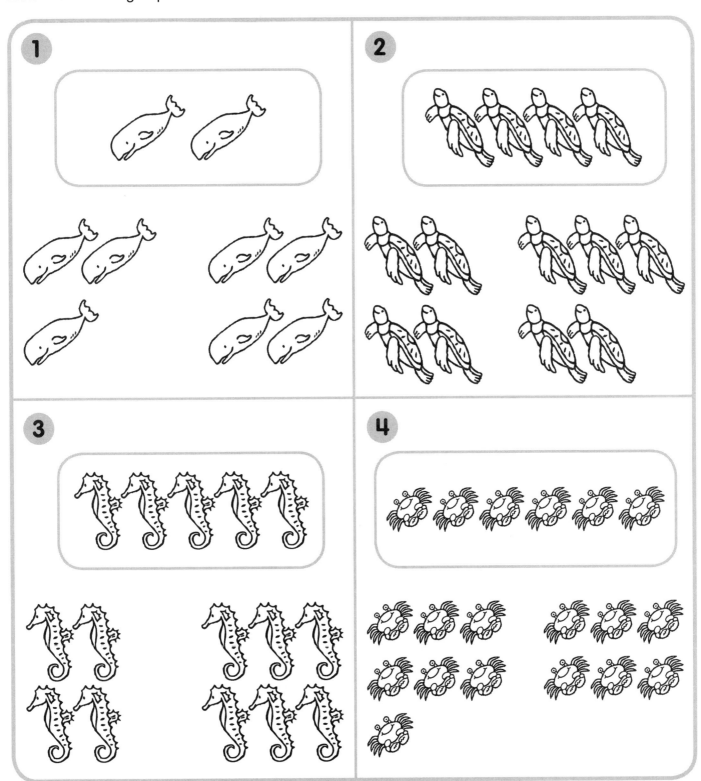

Name _____

What I Learned

What to Do
Have your child look at the picture. At the top, one crab faces forward. One more crab wants to join. Ask your child what happens when you add **1 more** crab. (Now there are 2 crabs.) Have your child trace the 2. Continue in this manner with the rest of the crabs.

WEEK 14

Home–School Connection

Math Concept: Addition is the operation of *adding to*.

To Parents
This week your child learned to add one more to a group.

What to Do Next
Place beans or other small objects in a bowl and play a counting game with your child. Begin by taking 4 beans. Then tell your child to take as many as you have plus **1 more**, and then count them aloud. Put the beans back in the bowl. Continue with different amounts up to 10.

Everyday Literacy: Math • EMC 3037 • © Evan-Moor Corp.

Concept

Subtraction is the operation of *taking from*.

Take Away One

Math Objective:

To help children understand the meaning of the operation of subtraction

Math Vocabulary:

altogether, left, one less, take away

Day 1 SKILLS

Number Sense

• Show an understanding of the quantity of one

• Understand that the final number counted in a set tells how many

• Understand that subtraction is *taking from*

Literacy

Oral Language Development

• Respond orally to simple questions

• Use number names

Comprehension

• Make connections using illustrations, prior knowledge, or real-life experiences

• Listen to a story being read aloud

Introducing the Concept

Use three blocks to model subtraction. Place the blocks on a table and say:

*Look at the blocks on the table. Count them with me: **1, 2, 3**. I will **take away** 1 block. Let's count to see how many blocks are left: **1, 2**. Three blocks **take away** 1 block are how many blocks?* (2 blocks)

Give each child 6 blocks. Lead children in repeating the process above by taking away 1 block from the 6 blocks, 5 blocks, and then the 4 blocks.

Listening to the Story

Distribute the Day 1 activity page. Say: *Listen and look at the pictures as I read a poem about insects. Cover one insect with your finger each time I say the words "Take away one."*

Five fuzzy flies
Shop at a store.
Take away one fly.
Now there are four.

Four thirsty ants
Sip some hot tea.
Take away one ant.
Now there are three.

Three moaning moths
Sick with the flu.
Take away one moth.
Now there are two.

Confirming Understanding

Distribute crayons. Develop the math concept by asking questions about the poem. Say:

• *Let's count the flies: **1, 2, 3, 4, 5**. Draw an **X** on one fly to take it away. Count how many flies are left: **1, 2, 3, 4**. Five flies **take away** 1 fly leaves how many flies?* (4)

• *Let's count the ants: **1, 2, 3, 4**. Draw an **X** on one ant to take it away. Count how many ants are left: **1, 2, 3**. Four ants **take away** 1 ant leaves how many ants?* (3)

Repeat the process with the moths.

Day 1 picture

Number Sense

- Show an understanding of the quantity of one
- Understand that the final number counted in a set tells how many
- Understand that subtraction is *taking from*

Literacy

Oral Language Development

- Respond orally to simple questions
- Use number names

Comprehension

- Recall details
- Make connections using illustrations, prior knowledge, or real-life experiences
- Make inferences and draw conclusions

Reinforcing the Concept

Reread the Day 1 poem. Then reinforce this week's math concept by guiding a discussion about the poem. Ask:

*What did we do to **take away** one?* (We covered an insect.)

Distribute the Day 2 activity and crayons. Say:

- *Point to box 1. How many ladybugs are there altogether?* (5) *Draw an **X** on one ladybug. How many ladybugs are **left**?* (4) *Circle the **4**.*

- *Point to box 2. How many butterflies are there?* (6) *Draw an **X** on one butterfly. How many butterflies are **left**?* (5) *Circle the **5**.*

- *Point to box 3. How many worms are there?* (8) *Draw an **X** on one worm. How many worms are **left**?* (7) *Circle the **7**.*

- *Point to box 4. How many ants are there?* (10) *Draw an **X** on one ant. How many ants are **left**?* (9) *Circle the **9**.*

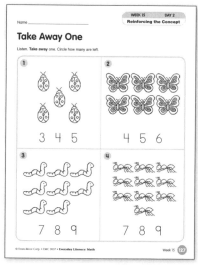

Day 2 activity

Number Sense

- Show an understanding of the quantity of one
- Understand that the final number counted in a set tells how many
- Understand that subtraction is *taking from*

Literacy

Oral Language Development

- Respond orally to simple questions
- Use number names

Comprehension

- Make connections using illustrations, prior knowledge, or real-life experiences

Applying the Concept

Distribute the Day 3 activity and crayons. Guide children through the activity by saying:

- *Point to the number 1. How many grasshoppers are in the first box?* (6) *Draw an **X** on one grasshopper. If you **take away** one grasshopper, how many grasshoppers will be left?* (5) *Circle the group with **5** grasshoppers.*

- *Look at row 2. How many ladybugs are in the first box?* (8) *Draw an **X** on one ladybug. If you **take away** 1 ladybug, how many ladybugs will be left?* (7) *Circle the group with **7** ladybugs.*

- *Look at row 3. How many moths are in the first box?* (7) *Draw an **X** on one moth. If you **take away** 1 moth, how many moths will be left?* (6) *Circle the group with **6** moths.*

- *Look at row 4. How many beetles are in the first box?* (10) *Draw an **X** on one beetle. If you **take away** 1 beetle, how many beetles will be left?* (9) *Circle the group with **9** beetles.*

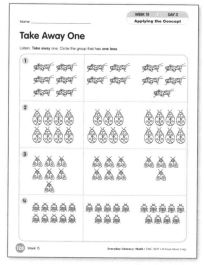

Day 3 activity

<table>
<tr>
<td>

Day 4
SKILLS

Number Sense
• Show an understanding of the quantity of one
• Understand that the final number counted in a set tells how many
• Understand that subtraction is *taking from*

Literacy

Oral Language Development
• Respond orally to simple questions
• Use number names

Comprehension
• Make connections using illustrations, prior knowledge, or real-life experiences

</td>
<td>

Extending the Concept

Distribute the Day 4 activity and crayons. Guide children through the activity by saying:

- *Point to picture 1. How many bees are there?* (3) *Circle the* **3** *under the bees.*

- *Now we are going to draw bees in the empty space. Draw a group with* **one less** *bee than* **3**. (children draw) *How many bees did you draw?* (2) *Circle the* **2** *under your drawing.*

- *Point to picture 2. How many ladybugs are there?* (5) *Circle the* **5** *under the ladybugs.*

- *Now draw a group with* **one less** *ladybug than* **5**. (children draw) *How many ladybugs did you draw?* (4) *Circle the* **4** *under your drawing.*

- *Point to picture 3. How many flowers are there?* (6) *Circle the* **6** *under the flowers.*

- *Now draw a group with* **one less** *flower than* **6**. (children draw) *How many flowers did you draw?* (5) *Circle the* **5** *under your drawing.*

</td>
</tr>
</table>

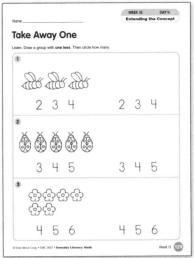

Day 4 activity

<table>
<tr>
<td>

Day 5
SKILLS

Number Sense
• Show an understanding of the quantity of one
• Understand that the final number counted in a set tells how many
• Understand that subtraction is *taking from*

Mathematical Thinking & Reasoning
• Explore mathematical ideas through song or play

Home-School Connection p. 130
Spanish version available (see p. 2)

</td>
<td>

Circle Time Math Activity

Reinforce this week's math concept with the following circle time activity:

Tell children that they will sing a finger play called "Ten Bugs in the Bed." Have children hold up all 10 fingers, which represent 10 bugs in one big bed. Teach children this song:

> ***Ten*** *bugs in the bed, and the little one said:*
> *"Roll over, roll over."*
> *So they all rolled over and one fell out.*

Children hold down one finger to represent the one bug that fell out of the bed.

Model mathematical thinking by saying, *We had 10 bugs, and 1 fell out. How many bugs are left?* (9) Continue playing by holding down one more finger after each verse:

> ***Nine*** *bugs in the bed, and the little one said:*
> *"Roll over, roll over."*
> *So they all rolled over and one fell out.*

When each child is holding up one last finger, sing:

> ***One*** *bug in the bed, and the little one said:*
> *"Good night!"*

</td>
<td>

</td>
</tr>
</table>

Name _____

Take Away One

Everyday Literacy: Math • EMC 3037 • © Evan-Moor Corp.

Name _____

Take Away One

Listen. **Take away** one. Circle how many are left.

1

3   4   5

2

4   5   6

3

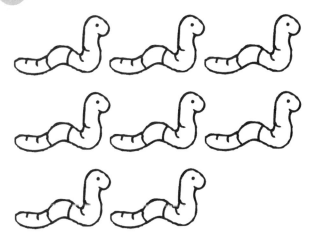

7   8   9

4

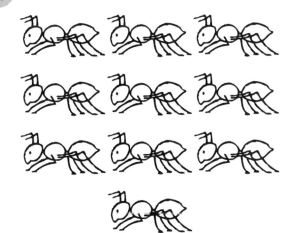

7   8   9

Name _____

Take Away One

Listen. **Take away** one. Circle the group that has **one less**.

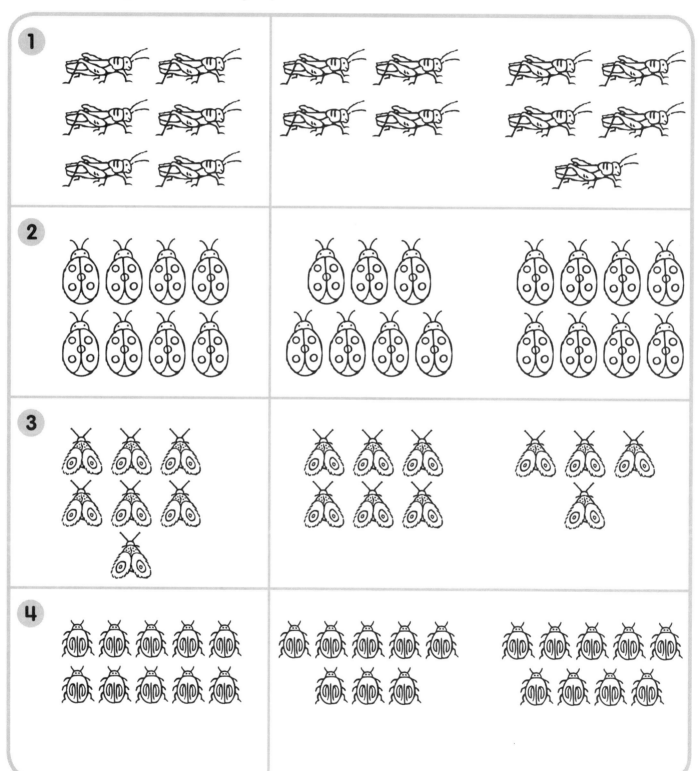

Name _____

Take Away One

Listen. Draw a group with **one less**. Then circle how many.

1

2   3   4   2   3   4

2

3   4   5   3   4   5

3

4   5   6   4   5   6

Name _____

What I Learned

What to Do

Have your child look at the pictures below. Ask him or her to count the insects in each row. Ask: *If I **take away** one fly, how many flies will I have left?* (4) Ask the same questions for the ants and the moths.

WEEK 15

Home–School Connection

Math Concept: Subtraction is the operation of *taking from.*

To Parents
This week your child learned to take away one from a group.

What to Do Next

Place beans or other small objects in a bowl and play a game of "One Less Bean" with your child. Take 6 beans and line them up on the table. Tell your child to form another line of beans, but with **one less** than 6. Continue lining up beans in varying amounts up to 10.

Everyday Literacy: Math • EMC 3037 • © Evan-Moor Corp.

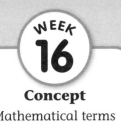

Concept
Mathematical terms are used to compare objects.

How Are They Different?

Math Objective:
To help children compare two objects and describe them in terms of mathematical properties

Math Vocabulary:
bigger/smaller, heavier/lighter, shorter/longer, different, same, shape, size

Day 1
SKILLS

Measurement
• Recognize the properties of length, size, and weight

Literacy

Oral Language Development
• Respond orally to simple questions
• Use mathematical terms

Comprehension
• Recall details
• Make connections using illustrations, prior knowledge, or real-life experiences
• Listen to a story being read aloud
• Make inferences and draw conclusions

Introducing the Concept

Begin the lesson by comparing the length of a crayon and a marker. Display the tools side by side and measure each from tip to tip. Say:

*Look at the marker from the cap to the point. Now look at the crayon from tip to end. Which is **longer**, the marker or the crayon? (marker) That's right. The marker is longer. Which is **shorter**? (crayon) That's right, the crayon is shorter than the marker.*

Listening to the Story

Distribute the Day 1 activity page. Say: *Listen and look at the picture as I read a story that tells how two dogs are different.*

Maddy's dogs are named Salt and Pepper. They look very different. First of all, they are different colors. Pepper has black fur, and Salt has white fur. In addition, they are different sizes. Pepper is bigger than Salt. Look at Salt's tail. It is longer than Pepper's tail. Salt also has longer ears than Pepper. Maddy's dogs are black and white, big and small, long and short. Maddy's dogs are very different, but she loves them both the same!

Confirming Understanding

Distribute crayons. Develop the math concept by asking children questions about the picture. Ask:

• *Which dog has a **shorter** tail?* (Pepper) *Circle Pepper's short tail.*

• *Circle the dog bed that is **smaller**. Why does Salt have a smaller bed than Pepper?* (Salt is smaller than Pepper.)

• *Which dog has **longer** ears?* (Salt) *Make a dot on each of Salt's long ears.*

Day 1 picture

Measurement

• Recognize the properties of length, size, and weight

Literacy

Oral Language Development

• Respond orally to simple questions

• Use mathematical terms

Comprehension

• Recall details

• Make connections using illustrations, prior knowledge, or real-life experiences

• Make inferences and draw conclusions

Reinforcing the Concept

Reread the Day 1 story. Reinforce this week's math concept by discussing the story. Say:

*Our story tells about two very different dogs. Which dog is **bigger**, Pepper or Salt? (Pepper)*

Distribute the Day 2 activity and crayons. Say:

- *Point to box 1. It shows two dogs. One dog is smaller than the other. Draw a circle around the dog that is **smaller**.*

- *Point to box 2. It shows two bones. Draw a line under the bone that is **longer**.*

- *Point to box 3. It shows two leashes. One leash is longer than the other. With a red crayon, draw a line next to the **shorter** leash. With a blue crayon, draw a line next to the **longer** leash.*

- *Point to box 4. It shows two dog bowls. One bowl is bigger than the other. Draw some dog food in the **bigger** bowl.*

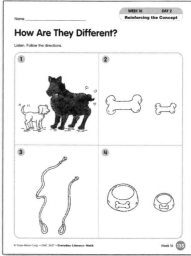

Day 2 activity

Measurement

• Recognize the properties of length, size, and weight

Geometry

• Recognize simple shapes, regardless of size or orientation

Literacy

Oral Language Development

• Respond orally to simple questions

• Use the names of basic shapes

Comprehension

• Make connections using illustrations, prior knowledge, or real-life experiences

Applying the Concept

Distribute the Day 3 activity and crayons. Then introduce the activity by saying:

A circle is a circle no matter what size it is. It can be a big circle or a small circle. This is true of all the other shapes. A square is a square even if it's big or small.

*Point to the shape in row 1. What is it? (circle) Draw a **smaller** circle next to it.*

- *Point to the **bigger** circle. Color it yellow.*

- *Point to the **smaller** circle. Color it red.*

*Point to the shape in row 2. What is it? (square) Draw a **bigger** square next to it.*

- *Point to the **bigger** square. Color it green.*

- *Point to the **smaller** square. Color it orange.*

*Point to the shape in row 3. What is it? (rectangle) Draw a **bigger** rectangle next to it.*

- *Point to the **bigger** rectangle. Color it purple.*

- *Point to the **smaller** rectangle. Color it red.*

*Point to the shape in row 4. What is it? (triangle) Draw a **bigger** triangle next to it.*

- *Point to the **bigger** triangle. Color it yellow.*

- *Point to the **smaller** triangle. Color it blue.*

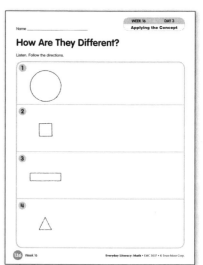

Day 3 activity

Day 4
SKILLS

Measurement
- Recognize the properties of length, size, and weight

Literacy

Oral Language Development
- Respond orally to simple questions
- Use mathematical terms

Comprehension
- Make connections using illustrations, prior knowledge, or real-life experiences
- Make inferences and draw conclusions

Extending the Concept

Distribute the Day 4 activity and crayons. Guide children through the activity by saying:

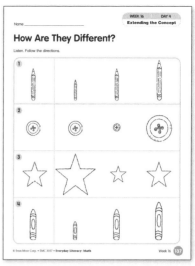

- *Point to row 1. The first picture shows a pencil. Color it yellow. Look at the other pencils. Find the pencil that is the **same size** as the first pencil. Color it yellow, too. Find the pencil that is **shorter** than the first pencil. Color it green.*

- *Point to row 2. The first picture shows a button. Color this first button red. Look at the other buttons. Find the button that is the **same size** as the first button. Color it red, too. Find the button that is **bigger** than the first button. Color it blue.*

- *Point to row 3. The first picture shows a star. Color this star orange. Look at the other stars. Find the star that is **bigger** than the first star. Color it red. Find the star that is **smaller** than the first star. Color it purple.*

- *Point to row 4. The first picture shows a crayon. Color this crayon any color. Look at the other crayons. Find the crayon that is the **same size** as the first crayon. Color it the same color as the first crayon. Find the crayon that is **longer** than the first crayon. Color it brown.*

Day 4 activity

Day 5
SKILLS

Measurement
- Recognize the properties of length, size, and weight

Literacy

Oral Language Development
- Use mathematical terms

Mathematical Thinking & Reasoning
- Select and use various types of reasoning and methods of proof

Home–School Connection p. 138
Spanish version available (see p. 2)

Hands-on Math Activity

Reinforce this week's math concept with the following hands-on activity:

Materials: index cards; two colors of yarn; crayons; palm-sized objects of similar shapes and sizes, but different weights. For example, rocks, ball of clay, ball of foil, bouncy ball, small inflated balloon, beanbag, orange, or apple.

Preparation: Use the index cards and yarn to make necklaces. Label half the necklaces "Researcher" and the other half "Tester." Make a testing station by placing the objects on a table. Place the crayons and extra index cards in a pile on the table.

Activity: Group children in pairs. Give each pair one of each necklace to wear, a crayon, and a blank index card. Explain that the researcher will point to two objects on the table and ask the tester to predict which one is heavier (or lighter). After the tester makes his or her prediction, the pair will test the prediction by having the tester hold one item in each hand to determine which item is heavier and which is lighter. If the tester's prediction was true, the researcher should draw a smiley face on the index card. If it was not true, the researcher should draw a sad face. After four or five experiments, have children switch necklaces.

Name _____

How Are They Different?

Name _____

How Are They Different?

Listen. Follow the directions.

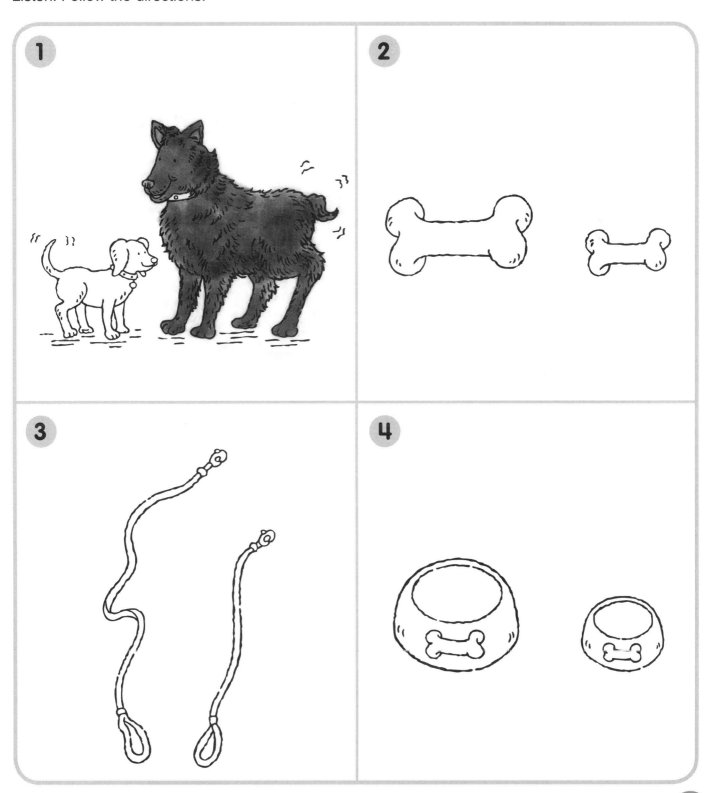

How Are They Different?

Listen. Follow the directions.

1

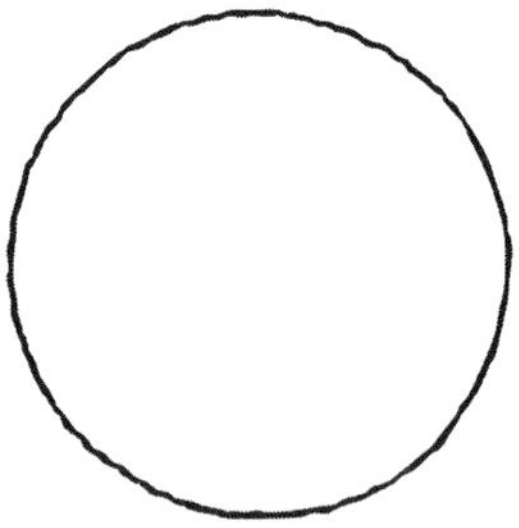

2

3

4

Everyday Literacy: Math • EMC 3037 • © Evan-Moor Corp.

Name _____

How Are They Different?

Listen. Follow the directions.

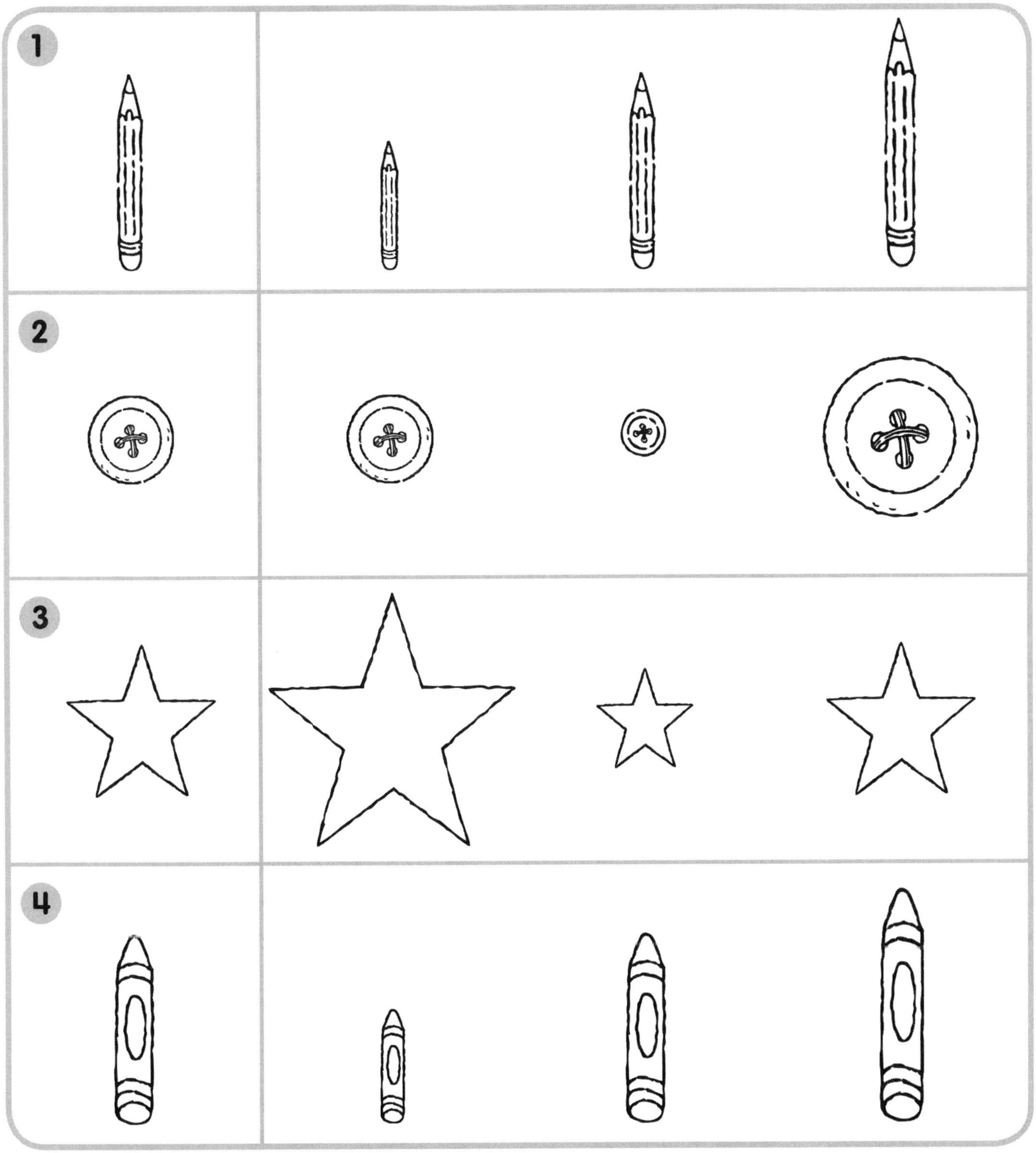

1	
2	
3	
4	

Name _____

What I Learned

What to Do
Have your child look at the picture below. Ask him or her to point out the differences between the two dogs. Ask questions that help your child use words such as *shorter, longer, bigger,* and *smaller.*

Math Concept: Mathematical terms are used to compare objects.

To Parents
This week your child learned to compare length, size, and weight.

What to Do Next
Use balls of play dough to compare length, size, and weight. Make dough balls of two different sizes, and guide your child in using words that compare their size and weight. From the dough balls, roll out two snakes of different lengths and have your child say which one is longer.

Let's Measure!

Math Objective:
To help children begin to use nonstandard units of measurement

Math Vocabulary:
length, long/longer, measure, same, short/shorter, tall

Day 1
SKILLS

Measurement
• Use a nonstandard unit to measure

Literacy

Oral Language Development
• Respond orally to simple questions
• Use number names

Comprehension
• Recall details
• Make connections using illustrations, prior knowledge, or real-life experiences
• Listen to a story being read aloud

Introducing the Concept

Prepare for the lesson by gathering books and linking cubes (or some other group of objects that can be used to model how to measure the length of a book). Say:

• *We can use objects to measure, or to tell how long or tall something is. Watch me measure this book. I will use cubes. I will start at one end of the book and link the cubes until I get to the other end.*

• *Let's count the cubes. (children count) This book is how many cubes long?* (children respond)

Then allow a child to help you model how to measure with nonstandard units of measure, such as long paper clips, blocks, or markers.

Listening to the Story

Distribute the Day 1 activity page. Say: *Listen and look at the picture as I read a story about how Kalia measured a bench in her garden.*

---

*Kalia wondered how long her garden bench was. Dad said that she could use her footsteps to find out. "My feet can measure?" asked Kalia. "Sure," said her dad. He showed her what to do. Kalia started at one end of the bench. She carefully placed one foot in front of the other. She counted each step as she walked from one end of the bench to the other: **1, 2, 3, 4, 5, 6, 7.** Kalia's bench was 7 footsteps long!*

Confirming Understanding

Develop the math concept by asking children questions about the story. Say:

• *Kalia wanted to measure her garden bench. What did she use to measure it?* (her footsteps)

• *Look at the flowers in front of the garden box. We can count these flowers to measure how long the box is. Let's count the flowers: **1, 2, 3, 4, 5, 6, 7.** How many flowers long is the box?* (7)

Day 1 picture

Measurement

• Use a nonstandard unit to measure

Literacy

Oral Language Development

• Respond orally to simple questions

• Use number names

Comprehension

• Recall details

• Make connections using illustrations, prior knowledge, or real-life experiences

Reinforcing the Concept

Reread the Day 1 story. Then reinforce this week's math concept by discussing the story. Say:

Kalia measured her bench using footsteps. What did we use to measure the box? (flowers) *Kalia also used other things to measure her bench.*

• *Look at row 1. Kalia measured her bench using flowerpots. How many flowerpots long is the bench?* (5) *That's right. The bench is **5** flowerpots long. Circle the number **5**.*

• *Look at row 2. Next, Kalia measured her bench using shovels. How many shovels long is the bench?* (3) *Yes, the bench is **3** shovels long. Circle the number **3**.*

• *Look at row 3. Finally, Kalia measured her bench using boots. How many boots long is the bench?* (6) *Yes, the bench is **6** boots long. Circle the number **6**.*

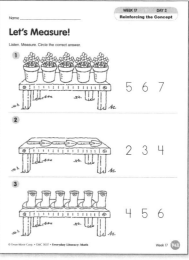

Day 2 activity

Measurement

• Use a nonstandard unit to measure

Literacy

Oral Language Development

• Respond orally to simple questions

• Use number names

Comprehension

• Recall details

• Make connections using illustrations, prior knowledge, or real-life experiences

Applying the Concept

Before beginning the activity, ensure that your paper clips match the outline on p. 144. If they do not, adjust the activity as needed.

Distribute the Day 3 activity and three large silver paper clips to each child. Introduce the activity by saying:

You can use many different things to find out how long something is, or to measure something. We will use paper clips to measure Kalia's flowers.

Model measuring the first flower as you say:

• *Point to the bottom of the first flower. Point to the paper clip shape on the line next to the flower. Place one paper clip on top of that paper clip shape. Add another paper clip right above the one you just placed. Add one more paper clip. The paper clips should be touching, with no space between them. Count the paper clips. How many paper clips tall is the first flower?* (3)

• *Point to the second flower. Place a paper clip on the line next to that flower, just as you did for the first one. Keep adding paper clips until you reach the top of the line. How many paper clips tall is the second flower?* (2)

• *Point to the third flower. Place a paper clip on the line next to that flower. How many paper clips tall is the third flower?* (1)

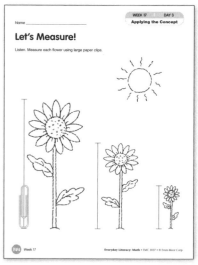

Day 3 activity

Measurement
• Use a nonstandard unit to measure

Literacy

Oral Language Development
• Respond orally to simple questions
• Use number names

Comprehension
• Make connections using illustrations, prior knowledge, or real-life experiences

Extending the Concept

Distribute the Day 4 activity, crayons, and three large silver paper clips to each child. Guide children through the activity by saying:

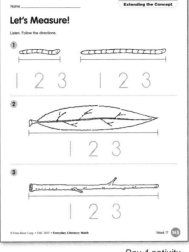

Day 4 activity

- *Look at the worms in row 1. Place one paper clip on the line below the first worm. How many paper clips long is the first worm? (1) Trace the number **1** under that worm.*

- *Now point to the second worm. Do you think this worm is **longer** or **shorter** than the first worm? (longer) Let's see if you are right. Lay one paper clip under the worm. Is this worm 1 paper clip long, or longer? (longer) Add another paper clip. How many paper clips long is the second worm? (2) That's right. This worm is 2 paper clips long. It's **longer** than the first worm. Trace the number **2** under the worm.*

- *Point to the leaf in row 2. Do you think this leaf is **longer** than, **shorter** than, or the **same** length as the stick in row 3? (same length) Let's see if you are right. First, measure the leaf using paper clips. How many paper clips long is the leaf? (3) Trace the number **3** under the leaf.*

- *Now measure the stick in row 3. How many paper clips long is it? (3) Trace the number **3** under the stick. Were you right? Is the leaf the **same** length as the stick? (yes) Yes, they are both 3 paper clips long.*

Measurement
• Use a nonstandard unit to measure

Literacy

Oral Language Development
• Use number names

Mathematical Thinking & Reasoning
• Select and use various types of reasoning and methods of proof

Home–School Connection p. 146
Spanish version available (see p. 2)

Hands-on Math Activity

Reinforce this week's math concept with the following hands-on activity:

Materials: large silver paper clips

Activity: Provide each child with 10 long paper clips. Link paper clips for children (or have them link the paper clips together, if they are able) to make a chain.

Next, suggest a variety of objects to measure that would be between 1 and 10 paper clips long (or tall). For example, have children measure a sheet of paper, cubbyhole, workbook, lunchbox, or framed photograph.

Have children predict how many paper clips each item measures. Then have them confirm by placing the chain against each item and counting the paper clips. Model mathematical thinking by making observations such as, *You measured this sheet of paper and found that it is about 6 paper clips long. Was your prediction true?*

Name _____

Let's Measure!

Name _____

Let's Measure!

Listen. Measure. Circle the correct answer.

1
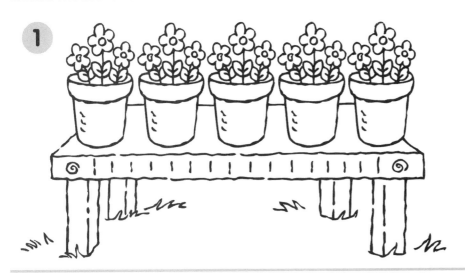

5   6   7

2
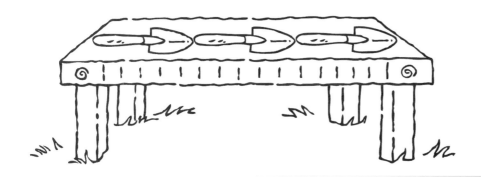

2   3   4

3
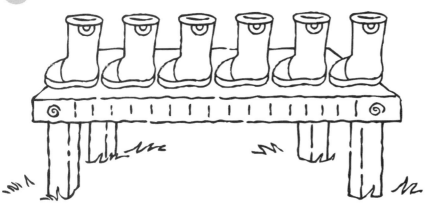

4   5   6

Name _____

Let's Measure!

Listen. Measure each flower using large paper clips.

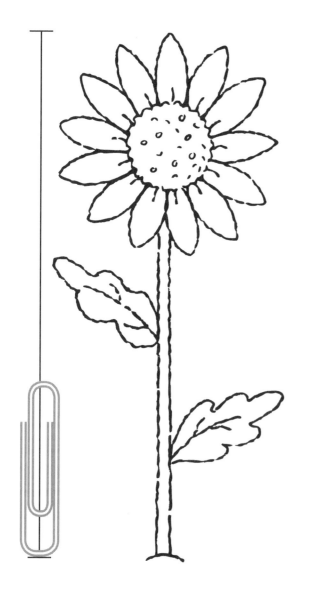

Name _____

Let's Measure!

Listen. Follow the directions.

1

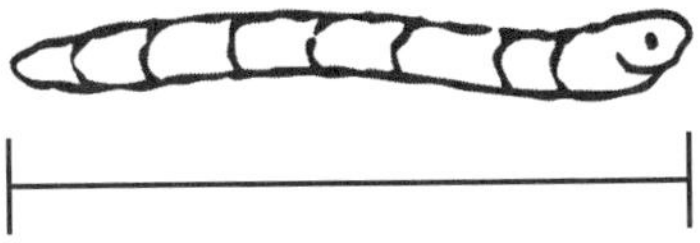

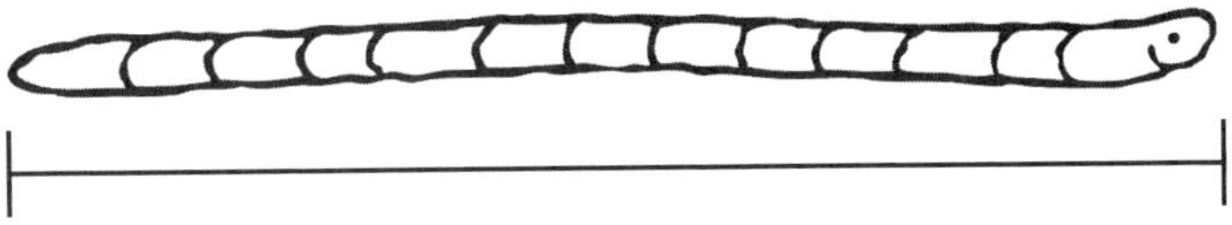

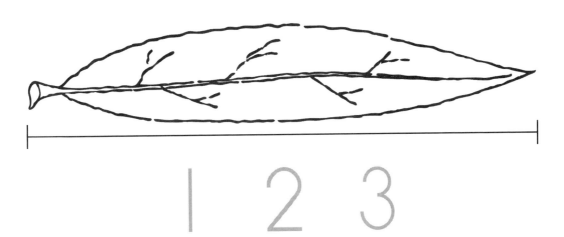

| 2 3 | 2 3

2

| 2 3

3

| 2 3

Name _____

What I Learned

What to Do

Have your child measure the flowers below using nonstandard units of measure, such as a small, standard-sized paper clips. Help your child place the nonstandard units on the line beside the flower. Then count how many units fit on the line. For example, write *about 4 small paper clips long* above the first flower.

Math Concept: Items may be measured using nonstandard units.

To Parents

This week your child learned to measure using nonstandard units.

What to Do Next

Measure the rooms in your home by using footsteps. Encourage your child to make predictions by asking questions such as, *How many footsteps do you think it will take to get from this wall to the door?*

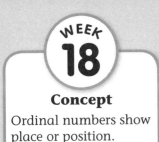

First in Line

Math Objective:
To help children develop an understanding of ordinal numbers

Math Vocabulary:
first, second, third, fourth, fifth, sixth, seventh, eighth, ninth, tenth, place, position

Day 1
SKILLS

Number Sense
• Identify relative place or position of objects in a sequence

Literacy

Oral Language Development
• Respond orally to simple questions
• Use number names

Comprehension
• Recall details
• Make connections using illustrations, prior knowledge, or real-life experiences
• Listen to a story being read aloud

Introducing the Concept

Begin by introducing the ordinal numbers **first** through **fifth**. The ordinal numbers **first**, **second**, **third**, and **fifth** differ from their corresponding cardinal numbers (1, 2, 3, and 5), so they may require extra practice. Say:

*We use special words to tell about position, or where something or someone is. For example, when you line up for recess, if you get there before anyone else, you might say "I'm **first**!" The person behind you is **second**. The words **first**, **second**, **third**, **fourth**, and **fifth** are called **ordinal numbers**.*

Once children are comfortable with the ordinals **first** through **fifth**, introduce **sixth** through **tenth**.

Listening to the Story

Distribute the Day 1 activity page. Say: *These 10 animals are in a parade. I will read a story that tells what place each animal is in.*

---

*Here comes the circus parade! Lion is proud to be **first**. Bear skates along in **second** place. Monkey is **third**, making all kinds of noise. Tiger is **fourth**. Hippo is **fifth**, walking gracefully on tippy-toes. Kangaroo hops along in **sixth** place. Camel enjoys being **seventh**. Zebra, who is **eighth**, shows off her stripes. Elephant is **ninth** and raises her trunk to say hello. Giraffe is **tenth**: the end of the line. He can see all the animals marching ahead. Hooray for the parade!*

Confirming Understanding

Distribute crayons. Develop the math concept by asking children questions about the picture. Ask:

• *How many animals are in the parade?* (10) *Which animal is **tenth**?* (Giraffe) *Draw an X on Giraffe.*

• *Circle the animal that is **second**. Which animal did you circle?* (Bear)

• *Make a red dot on the camel. Which number word tells the place Camel is in?* (seventh)

• *Which is the **sixth** animal?* (Kangaroo)

Day 1 picture

Day 2
SKILLS

Number Sense

- Identify relative place or position of objects in a sequence

Literacy

Oral Language Development

- Respond orally to simple questions
- Use number names

Comprehension

- Recall details
- Make connections using illustrations, prior knowledge, or real-life experiences

Reinforcing the Concept

Reread the Day 1 story. Then reinforce this week's math concept by guiding a discussion about the story. Say:

*Our story was about a parade. Who was the **first** animal? (Lion) Who was the **tenth**? (Giraffe)*

Distribute the Day 2 activity and crayons. Say:

- *Point to box 1. The circus animals have changed places. I see Tiger, Camel, and Monkey. Is Monkey the **second** animal in line? Color the happy face for **yes** or the sad face for **no**. (no) What number is he in line? (third)*

- *Point to box 2. Here are Giraffe, Monkey, and Bear. Is Monkey the **second** animal in line? Color the happy face for **yes** or the sad face for **no**. (yes)*

- *Point to box 3. Here are Elephant, Giraffe, and Lion. Is Elephant the **third** animal in line? Color the happy face for **yes** or the sad face for **no**. (no) What number is she in line? (first)*

- *Point to box 4. Now we have four animals: Bear, Dog, Elephant, and Monkey. Is Monkey the **fourth** animal in line? Color the happy face for **yes** or the sad face for **no**. (yes)*

Day 2 activity

Day 3
SKILLS

Number Sense

- Identify relative place or position of objects in a sequence

Literacy

Oral Language Development

- Respond orally to simple questions
- Use number names

Comprehension

- Make connections using illustrations, prior knowledge, or real-life experiences
- Make inferences and draw conclusions

Applying the Concept

Distribute the Day 3 activity and crayons. Then introduce the activity by saying:

*Number words like **first**, **second**, **third**, **fourth**, and **fifth** tell where something is in a line.*

- *The animals are ready to show their tricks at the circus. Look at the flags. Point to each one as we count: **1, 2, 3, 4, 5, 6, 7, 8**.*

- *Point to the **third** flag. Color it blue. Point to the **sixth** flag. Color it green. Point to the **eighth** flag. Color it red.*

- *The monkey is juggling balls. How many balls is he juggling? (6) Point to the **first** ball. Color it yellow. Point to the **fourth** ball. Color it green.*

- *Look at the seal with the balloons. How many balloons are there? (5) Point to the **second** balloon. Make a red dot on it. Point to the **fourth** balloon. Make a blue dot on it. Point to the **fifth** balloon. Make a purple dot on it. Draw a **sixth** balloon. Make a green dot on the **sixth** balloon.*

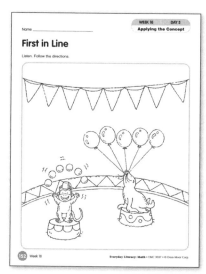

Day 3 activity

Everyday Literacy: Math • EMC 3037 • © Evan-Moor Corp.

Number Sense

• Identify relative place or position of objects in a sequence

Literacy

Oral Language Development

• Respond orally to simple questions

• Use number names

Comprehension

• Make connections using illustrations, prior knowledge, or real-life experiences

Applying the Concept

Distribute the Day 4 activity and crayons. Guide children through the activity by saying:

Here are some things you might see at a circus. Let's start with the clowns.

Day 4 activity

- *Put your finger on row 1. How many clowns are there? (4) Draw a circle around the **third** clown. Now draw a line under the **fourth** clown.*

- *Put your finger on row 2. These are circus performers. The **first** one is a seal. What is the **second** one? (a dog) What is the **third** one? (a bear) Draw a circle around the **second** performer.*

- *Put your finger on row 3. These are tightrope walkers. The **second** one is an elephant. The **first** one is a hippo. What is the **third** one? (a monkey) Draw a circle around the **third** tightrope walker.*

- *Put your finger on row 4. These are snacks you might buy at a circus. Make a dot on the **second** snack. What is the **second** snack? (ice-cream cone) Draw a circle around the **fourth** snack. What is the **fourth** snack? (hot dog) Draw a line under the **third** snack. What is the **third** snack? (peanuts) Draw an **X** on the **first** snack. What is the **first** snack? (popcorn)*

Number Sense

• Identify relative place or position of objects in a sequence

Literacy

Oral Language Development

• Use number names

Mathematical Thinking & Reasoning

• Explore mathematical ideas through song or play

Home–School Connection p. 154
Spanish version available (see p. 2)

Circle Time Math Activity

Reinforce this week's math concept with the following circle time activity:

Preparation: Practice the song below to the tune of "I'm a Little Teapot."

Activity: Tell children they will be in a circus parade, pretending to be a monkey, tiger, elephant, hippo, camel, lion, giraffe, penguin, seal, and pony.

Assign each child a role and a position in the parade. For example, say, *You are a monkey and you are first.* Have children join the parade as their name is called. Keeping in mind the particular way each animal moves, have children follow the commands in the song:

*I'm a little monkey, **first** in line.*
I move like this all the time.
When I'm feeling happy, I will hop,
twirl around, and then I'll drop.

*I'm a little tiger, **second** in line.*
I move like this all the time.
When I'm feeling happy, I will hop,
twirl around, and then I'll drop.

Name _____

First in Line

Name _____

First in Line

Listen. Color the happy face for **yes**. Color the sad face for **no**.

Name _____

First in Line

Listen. Follow the directions.

Everyday Literacy: Math • EMC 3037 • © Evan-Moor Corp.

Name _____

First in Line

Listen. Follow the directions.

Name _____

What I Learned

What to Do
Have your child look at the picture below. Ask him or her to use ordinal numbers *(first, second, third, fourth, fifth, sixth, seventh, eighth, ninth, tenth)* to tell you what place each animal is in.

What to Do Next
Practice ordinal numbers with a box of animal crackers. Select one cracker of each type of animal and help your child identify each one. Then have your child arrange the animal crackers in a line, as in a parade. Ask questions such as, *Which animal is in third place? in fifth place?*

Find the Answer

Math Objective:

To help children learn strategies for solving word problems

Math Vocabulary:

add, altogether, answer, in all, left, less, more, solve, story problem, take away

---

Day 1
SKILLS

Number Sense

• Use numbers and counting to solve word problems

Literacy

Oral Language Development

• Respond orally to simple questions

• Use mathematical terms

• Use number names

Comprehension

• Recall details

• Make connections using illustrations, prior knowledge, or real-life experiences

• Listen to a story being read aloud

Introducing the Concept

Prepare for the lesson by having a box of crayons and a sheet of paper handy. Then narrate (do <u>not</u> model) a simple addition story problem:

I am going to tell you a story. I have 3 crayons. I take 2 more crayons from the box. How many crayons do I have now? (5) *The story I just told you is called a story problem. You imagined the crayons and figured out the answer. Let's solve the story problem in another way.*

Model solving the problem using actual crayons:

*Let's use real crayons to find the answer. Here are the 3 crayons I started with: **1, 2, 3**. I will take two more: **1, 2**. Count all the crayons together: **1, 2, 3, 4, 5**. The answer is **5**. We were right! Now we'll draw the story problem.*

Next, use a sheet of paper to solve the problem using pictures:

*Now let's solve the story problem by drawing pictures of crayons. I will draw 3 crayons: **1, 2, 3**. Next, I will draw 2 more. Let's count the crayons: **1, 2, 3, 4, 5**. The answer is **5**.*

Listening to the Story

Distribute the Day 1 activity page. Say: *Listen and look at the picture as I read a story about a teacher who gets one more flower.*

Today is Miss Olson's birthday. The children gave her 4 flowers, which Miss Olson placed in a vase. Daniel came in with 1 more flower for Miss Olson. "How pretty!" said Miss Olson. "There are 4 flowers in the vase. Now I will add 1 more. Thank you, Daniel."

Confirming Understanding

Distribute crayons. Develop the math concept by asking children questions about the story. Say:

Day 1 picture

• *Miss Olson had 4 flowers. She got 1 more. How many flowers does Miss Olson have?* (5) *Yes, the answer is 5.*

• *Here is another way to find the answer. In the box, draw dots instead of flowers. Draw 4 dots and 1 dot. How many dots are there in all?* (5)

• *You can also use your fingers to find the answer. Hold up 4 fingers. Add another finger for the flower that Daniel brought. How many fingers are you holding up?* (5)

Day 2
SKILLS

Number Sense

• Use numbers and counting to solve word problems

Literacy

Oral Language Development

• Respond orally to simple questions

• Use mathematical terms

• Use number names

Comprehension

• Recall details

• Make connections using illustrations, prior knowledge, or real-life experiences

Reinforcing the Concept

Reread the Day 1 story. Then reinforce this week's math concept by discussing the story. Say:

Miss Olson had 4 flowers. She received 1 more. How many flowers did she have in all? (5) *How did we find the answer? (by counting; by adding 1 flower to 4 flowers)*

Distribute the Day 2 activity and crayons. Say:

• *Point to row 1. Miss Olson has 3 flowers. Tyler gave her 3 more flowers. How many flowers does Miss Olson have altogether?* (6) *Trace the number* **6**.

• *Point to row 2. Miss Olson collected 4 apples after snack time. Then she found 3 more apples on the table. How many apples does she have in all?* (7) *Trace the number* **7**.

• *Point to row 3. Zach was coloring with 5 crayons. He found 3 more crayons under his chair. How many crayons does Zach have now?* (8) *Trace the number* **8**.

• *Point to row 4. Mari was building with blocks. She had 5 blocks. Zach gave her 4 more blocks. How many blocks does Mari have now?* (9) *Trace the number* **9**.

Day 2 activity

Day 3
SKILLS

Number Sense

• Use numbers and counting to solve word problems

Literacy

Oral Language Development

• Respond orally to simple questions

• Use mathematical terms

• Use number names

Comprehension

• Recall details

• Make connections using illustrations, prior knowledge, or real-life experiences

Applying the Concept

Use crayons to review the concept of addition and to introduce the concept of subtraction. Say:

When you **add** *to a group, you get* **more***. When you* **take away** *from a group, you have* **less***. I will show you.*

I have 5 crayons. One of my students needs 1 crayon, so I give it to her. Now how many crayons do I have? (4) *Yes, now I have 4 crayons. I have* **less** *crayons.*

Distribute the Day 3 activity and crayons. Say:

• *Point to row 1. Zach's mom baked 6 cookies. Zach ate 2 of them.* **Take away** *the 2 cookies by tracing the* **X** *on them. How many cookies are left?* (4) *Trace the number* **4**.

• *Point to row 2. Miss Olson had 6 flowers. After a few days, 1 flower died, so she took it out of the vase.* **Take away** *the dead flower by tracing the* **X** *on it. How many flowers are left?* (5) *Trace the number* **5**.

• *Point to row 3. Mari's tower had 9 blocks. When it got too tall, 3 blocks fell off.* **Take away** *the 3 blocks that fell off. Trace the* **X** *on them. How many blocks are still standing?* (6) *Trace the number* **6**.

• *Point to row 4. There were 4 apples on the snack table. Kara and Zach ate 2 of them.* **Take away** *2 apples. Trace the* **X** *on them. How many apples are left?* (2) *Trace the number* **2**.

Day 3 activity

Everyday Literacy: Math • EMC 3037 • © Evan-Moor Corp.

Number Sense

• Use numbers and counting to solve word problems

Literacy

Oral Language Development

• Respond orally to simple questions

• Use mathematical terms

• Use number names

Comprehension

• Recall details

• Make connections using illustrations, prior knowledge, or real-life experiences

Extending the Concept

Distribute the Day 4 activity and crayons. Guide children through the activity by saying:

Day 4 activity

- *Point to row 1. Henry had 6 crayons on his desk. One crayon fell off his desk. That means you need to **take away** 1 crayon. Draw an **X** on 1 crayon. How many crayons does Henry have left? (5) Trace the number 5.*

- *Point to row 2. Zach saw 2 birds sitting on a branch. Two more birds flew onto the branch. That means you need to **add** the birds. Count all the birds. How many are there altogether? (4) Trace the number 4.*

- *Point to row 3. Emma blew 5 bubbles into the air. Two bubbles popped. Will you **take away** 2 bubbles, or will you **add** 2 bubbles? (take away) That's right. Draw an **X** on 2 bubbles. How many bubbles are still in the air? (3) Trace the number 3.*

- *Point to row 4. Max collects rocks. Yesterday he found 2 shiny rocks. Today he found 3 rough rocks. Will you **add** 3 rocks, or will you **take away** 3 rocks? (add) That's right. Count all the rocks. How many rocks does Max have altogether? (5) Trace the number 5.*

Number Sense

• Use numbers and counting to solve word problems

Literacy

Oral Language Development

• Use mathematical terms

• Use number names

Mathematical Thinking & Reasoning

• Use math to solve problems

Home–School Connection p. 162

Spanish version available (see p. 2)

Hands-on Math Activity

Reinforce this week's math concept with the following hands-on activity:

Materials: 10 empty plastic bottles with tops, playground ball

Preparation: Fill the bottles halfway with water for stability. Arrange the bottles in a standard 10-pin layout.

Activity: Have children take turns bowling, knocking down the bottles with the ball.

As children bowl, translate each real-life scenario into a story problem. For example, say: *Ten bottles were standing. Maya knocked down 3 of them. How many bottles are still standing? (7)*

Encourage children to solve the problem by physically counting the bottles still standing or by using their fingers to represent the bottles.

Before setting up the bottles again, use the opportunity to model the inverse addition problem. For example, say: *Seven bottles are standing. I will add 3 more bottles. How many bottles are standing now? (10)*

Name _____

Find the Answer

Name _____

Find the Answer

Listen. Trace the correct answer.

1   4 5 6

2   6 7 8

3 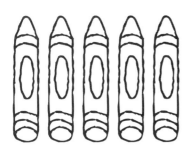 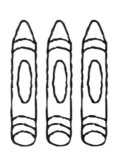 7 8 9

4 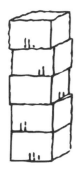 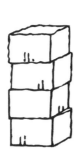 8 9 10

Name _____

Find the Answer

Listen. Trace the correct answer.

1

4 5 6

2

3 4 5

3

6 7 8

4

2 3 4

Name _____

Find the Answer

Listen. Trace the correct answer.

1

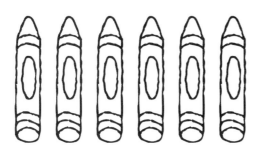

4 5 6

2

2 3 4

3

 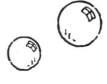

2 3 4

4

   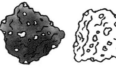

4 5 6

Name _____

What I Learned

WEEK 19

Home–School Connection

What to Do
Have your child look at the picture below. Ask him or her to count the flowers in the vase. Then point to the flower that the boy is holding. Ask your child to draw dots in the box to show the story problem. (4 dots and 1 dot) Ask: *How many flowers are there altogether?* (5) Finally, have your child color the picture.

Math Concept: Word problems may be solved in many ways.

To Parents
This week your child learned to solve simple addition and subtraction problems.

What to Do Next
Practice simple word problems with your child by using cereal rings. For example, say, *You have 5 cereal rings. I give you 2 cereal rings. How many cereal rings do you have now?* (7) Then have your child come up with a simple word problem for you to solve.

Everyday Literacy: Math • EMC 3037 • © Evan-Moor Corp.

WEEK
20
Concept
Data can be organized
on a graph.

Graphs

Math Objective:
To help children collect, organize, and record data

Math Vocabulary:
box, column, count, graph, row

Day 1
SKILLS

Number Sense
• Understand the
relationship between
numbers and quantities

Data Analysis
• Collect, organize, and
record data

Literacy

**Oral Language
Development**
• Respond orally to simple
questions
• Use number names

Comprehension
• Recall details
• Make connections
using illustrations, prior
knowledge, or real-life
experiences
• Listen to a story being
read aloud

Introducing the Concept

Prepare for the lesson by making a graph with two rows. Divide each row
into boxes, until the graph has one box for each child. Label one row with
a drawing of a pair of white socks and the other with a crossed-out pair
of white socks. Say:

*This is a graph. A graph helps us see how much of something there
is. Let's use this graph to tell us about our socks. Let's begin. Are
you wearing white socks? If so, raise your hand.* (children respond)

Together, count the children wearing white socks. Record the number by
coloring in the corresponding number of boxes in the white sock row.
Do the same for the children wearing colored socks or no socks. Then say:

*The graph is finished. Which row has more boxes filled in, children
wearing white socks or colored socks or no socks?* (children respond)

Listening to the Story

Distribute the Day 1 activity page. Say: *Look at the picture and listen as
I read about Abby, a girl who made a graph.*

---

*Abby wanted to know what kinds of pets her friends had. She
decided to make a graph. She made one row for cats and one row
for dogs. She asked her friends, "Do you have a cat or a dog?" She
counted how many friends had cats. She colored the boxes in the cat
row. Then she counted how many friends had dogs. She colored the
boxes in the dog row. She looked at her graph and said, "Most of my
friends are dog lovers!"*

Confirming Understanding

Develop the math concept by focusing attention
on the graph. Ask:

• *What does Abby's graph show?* (how
many cats and dogs Abby's friends have)

• *How many of Abby's friends have cats?* (2)

• *How many of Abby's friends have dogs?* (5)

• *Do more friends have cats or dogs?* (dogs)

Day 1 picture

Day 2
SKILLS

Number Sense
- Understand the relationship between numbers and quantities

Data Analysis
- Collect, organize, and record data

Literacy

Oral Language Development
- Respond orally to simple questions
- Use number names

Comprehension
- Recall details
- Make connections using illustrations, prior knowledge, or real-life experiences

Reinforcing the Concept

Reread the Day 1 story. Then reinforce this week's math concept by discussing the story. Ask:

Did Abby's graph show more friends with cats or more friends with dogs? (with dogs) *Abby's graph was about two types of pets. We are going to make a graph about three types of socks.*

Distribute the Day 2 activity and crayons. Say:

- *All these socks just came out of the dryer. We need to count each kind of sock. First, count the dark socks.* (children count) *How many dark socks are there?* (4) *Find the row with the dark sock next to it. There are **4** dark socks, so color **4** boxes in the dark sock row.*

- *Next, count the striped socks.* (children count) *How many striped socks are there?* (3) *On the graph, find the row with the striped sock. There are **3** striped socks, so color **3** boxes in the striped sock row.*

- *Finally, count the white socks.* (children count) *How many white socks are there?* (5) *On the graph, find the row with the white sock. There are **5** white socks, so color **5** boxes in the white sock row.*

- *Look at your graph. Are there more white socks or dark socks?* (white socks) *Are there more dark socks or striped socks?* (dark socks)

Day 2 activity

Day 3
SKILLS

Number Sense
- Understand the relationship between numbers and quantities

Data Analysis
- Collect, organize, and record data

Literacy

Oral Language Development
- Respond orally to simple questions
- Use number names

Comprehension
- Make connections using illustrations, prior knowledge, or real-life experiences

Reinforcing the Concept

Distribute the Day 3 activity and crayons. Guide children through the activity by saying:

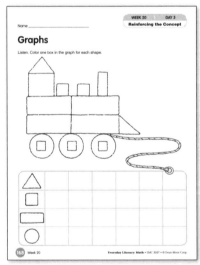

- *Look at the toy train. What shapes do you see?* (triangles, squares, rectangles, circles) *Let's make a graph to show how many of each shape there are.*

- *First, count the triangles on the train. How many triangles are there?* (2) *Now point to the triangle on the graph. Use green to color **2** boxes in the triangle row.*

- *Now count the squares on the train. How many squares are there?* (6) *Now point to the square on the graph. Use red to color **6** boxes in the square row.*

- *Next, count the rectangles on the train. How many rectangles are there?* (5) *Now point to the rectangle on the graph. Use orange to color **5** boxes in the rectangle row.*

- *Last, count the circles on the train. How many circles are there?* (3) *Point to the circle on the graph. Use blue to color **3** boxes in that row.*

Model how to read the graph, starting at each shape and moving across each row.

Day 3 activity

Number Sense
- Understand the relationship between numbers and quantities

Data Analysis
- Collect, organize, and record data

Literacy

Oral Language Development
- Respond orally to simple questions
- Use number names

Comprehension
- Make connections using illustrations, prior knowledge, or real-life experiences

Extending the Concept

Distribute the Day 4 activity and crayons. Introduce the activity by saying:

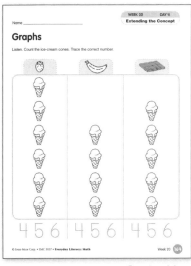

Day 4 activity

> *We made graphs that use boxes and rows to tell us how many. Here is a new type of graph. It uses columns. We read it from top to bottom.*

> *A teacher asked her students which ice-cream flavors they liked best. She made this graph to show how many children liked each flavor.*

- *Look at the graph. Color the strawberry and all of the ice-cream cones in the column pink.*

- *Now count the strawberry ice-cream cones. How many children like strawberry ice cream best?* (6) *Trace the number **6**.*

- *Look at the next column on the graph. Color the banana and all of the ice-cream cones below it yellow.*

- *Now count the banana ice-cream cones. How many children like banana ice cream best?* (4) *Trace the number **4**.*

- *Look at the last column on the graph. Color the chocolate bar and all of the ice-cream cones below it brown.*

- *Now count the chocolate ice-cream cones. How many children like chocolate ice cream best?* (5) *Trace the number **5**.*

Number Sense
- Understand the relationship between numbers and quantities

Data Analysis
- Collect, organize, and record data

Literacy

Oral Language Development
- Use number names

Mathematical Thinking & Reasoning
- Select and use various types of reasoning and methods of proof

Home–School Connection p. 170
Spanish version available (see p. 2)

Hands-on Math Activity

Reinforce this week's math concept with the following hands-on activity:

Materials: chart paper, crayons in primary colors, 3" x 3" white self-adhesive notes (one note per child)

Preparation: Draw a grid with 8 rows, one for each of the colors in a standard box of crayons: red, orange, yellow, blue, green, purple, brown, black. Label each row with its matching colored circle.

Activity: Tell children that you will make a class graph that shows favorite colors. Place children in small groups and have them share crayons. Give each child a self-adhesive note, and ask him or her to draw a circle and color it in their favorite color.

After children have finished coloring their circles, graph the results. Ask, *Who drew a red circle?* Have those children come up and place their red circle sticky notes in the red row.

Continue with the other colored circles. Have children count the total number of circles per color. Analyze the results by asking questions such as, *Which color do the most children like?* (children respond) *How do you know?* (That color has the most sticky notes.)

Name _____

Graphs

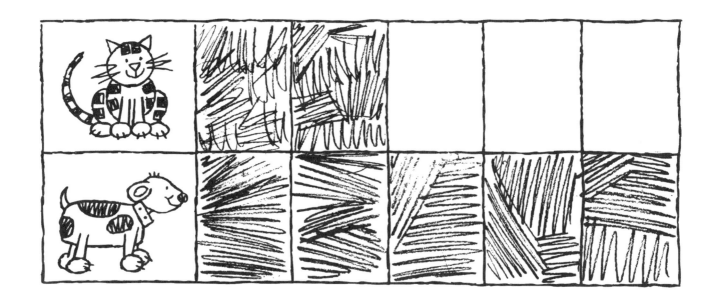

Name _____

Graphs

Listen. Color one box in the graph for each sock.

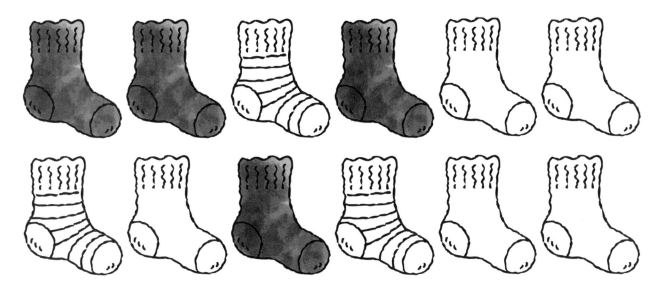

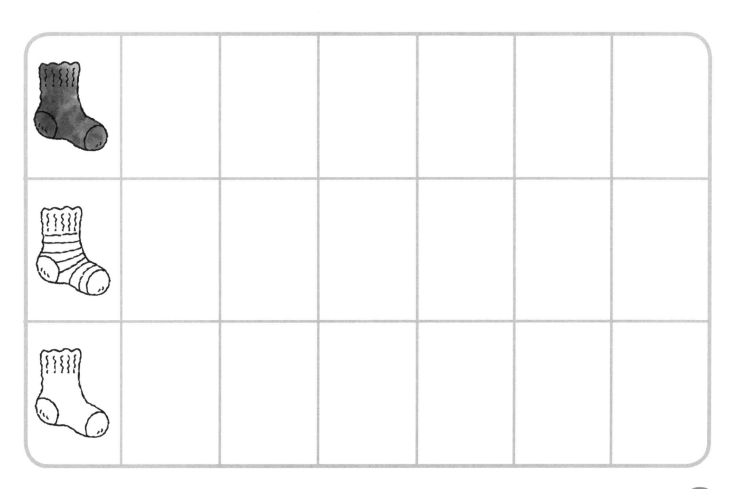

Name _____

Graphs

Listen. Color one box in the graph for each shape.

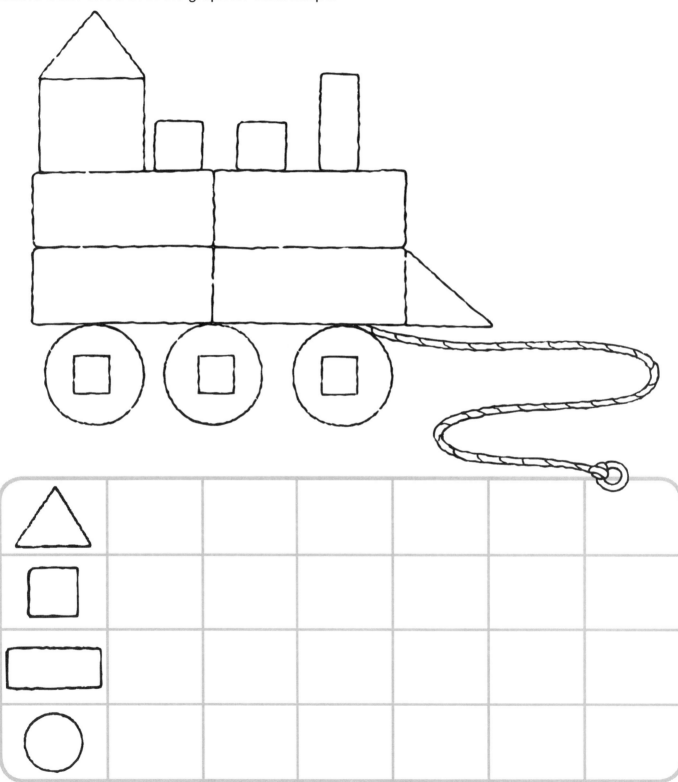

Everyday Literacy: Math • EMC 3037 • © Evan-Moor Corp.

Name _____

Graphs

Listen. Count the ice-cream cones. Trace the correct number.

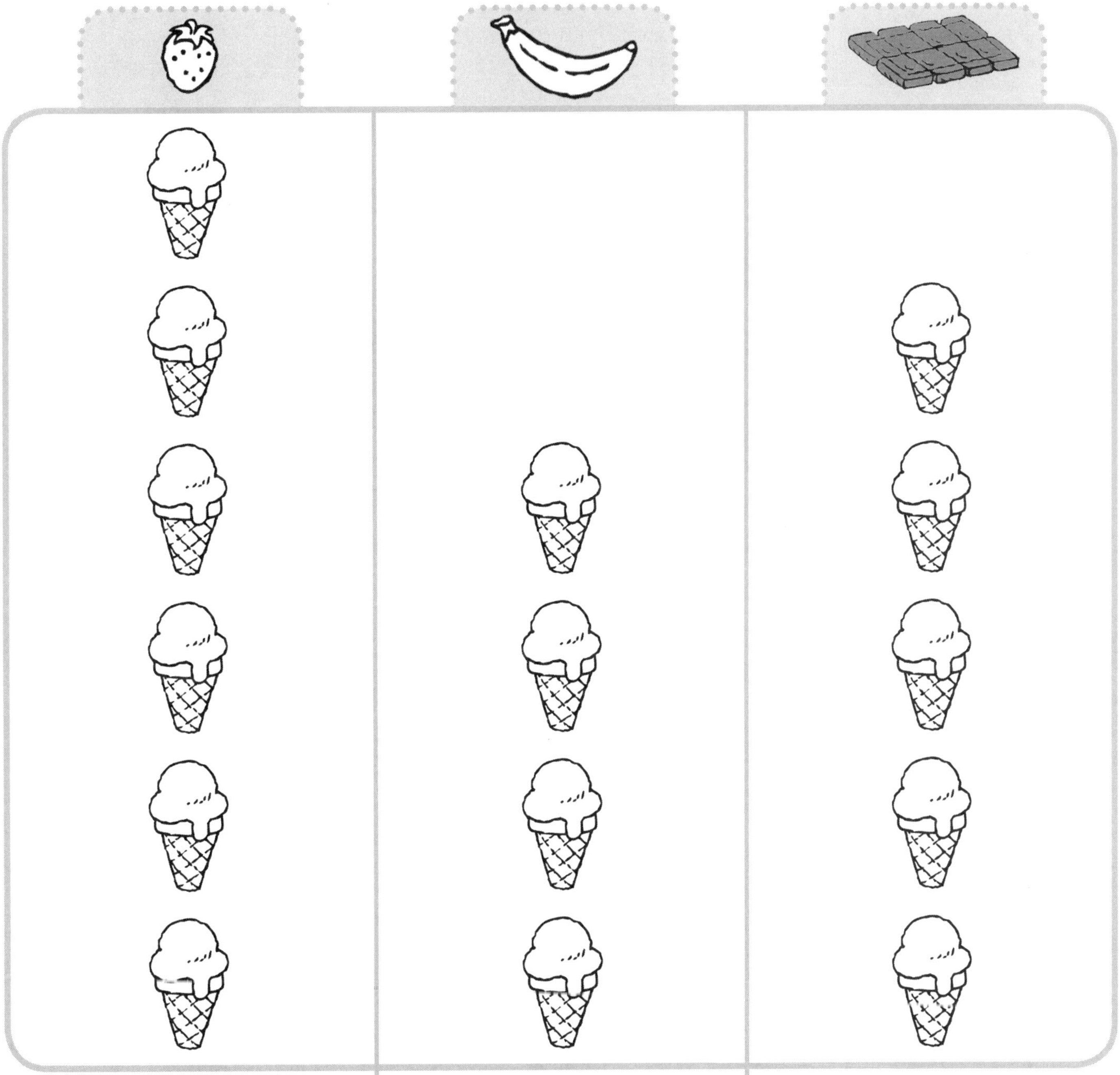

4 5 6 | 4 5 6 | 4 5 6

Name _____

What I Learned

WEEK 20

Home–School Connection

Math Concept: Data can be organized on a graph.

To Parents
This week your child learned to graph data.

What to Do

Have your child describe the various socks pictured below (dark, white, and striped). Then help your child color in the graph to show how many of each sock there are. Analyze the results by asking questions such as, *Are there more dark socks than white socks?* (no) *How many striped socks are there?* (3)

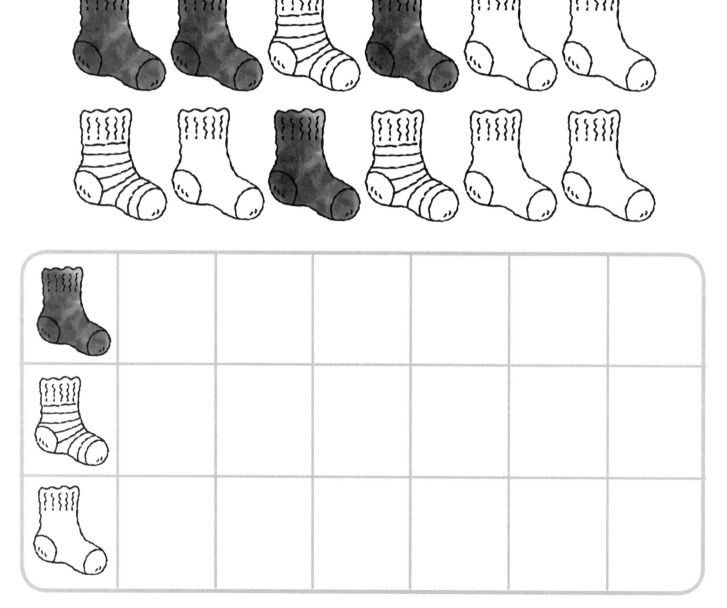

What to Do Next

Lay out real socks for your child to sort and graph. On a sheet of paper, prepare a graph similar to the one above, labeling each row accordingly. Then have your child color a box for each sock.

Everyday Literacy: Math • EMC 3037 • © Evan-Moor Corp.

Answer Key

Week 1

Day 1

Day 2

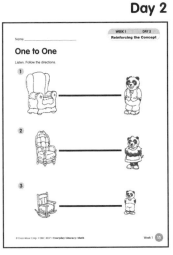

Day 3

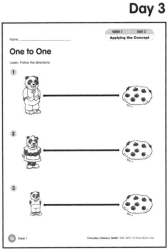

Day 4

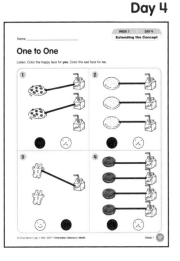

Week 2

Day 1

Day 2

Day 3

Day 4

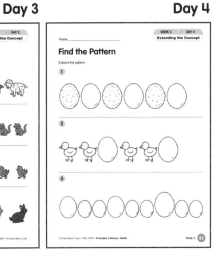

Week 3

Day 1

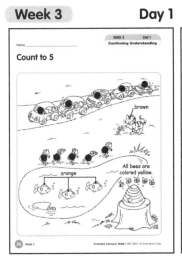

Day 2

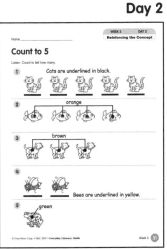

Day 3

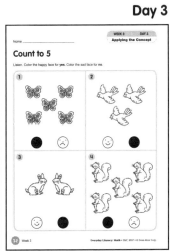

Day 4

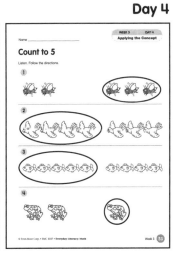

Week 4

Day 1

Day 2

Day 3

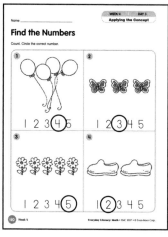

Day 4

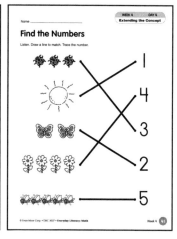

Week 5

Day 1

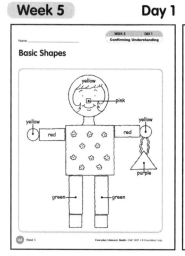

Day 2

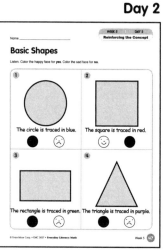

Day 3

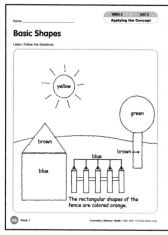

Day 4

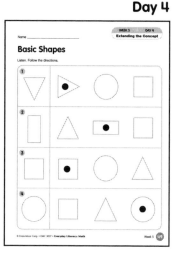

Week 6

Day 1

Day 2

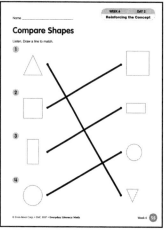

Day 3

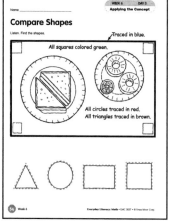

Day 4

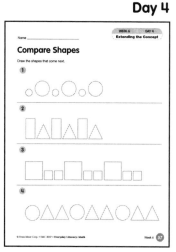

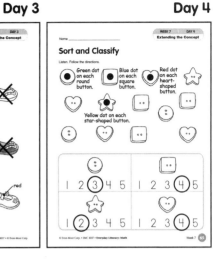

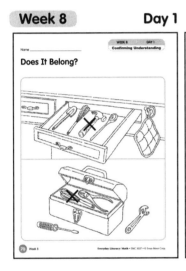

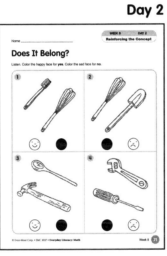

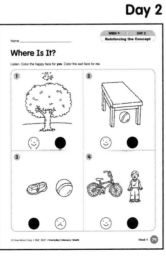

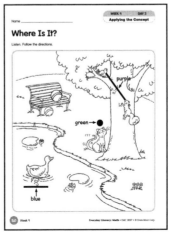

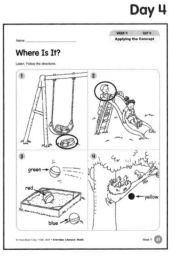

Week 10

Day 1

Day 2

Day 3

Day 4

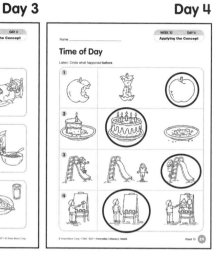

Week 11

Day 1

Day 2

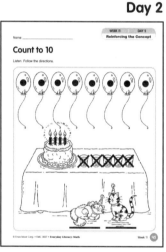

Day 3

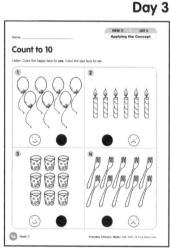

Day 4

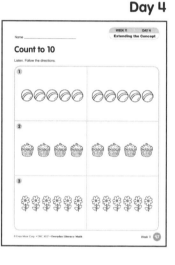

Week 12

Day 1

Day 2

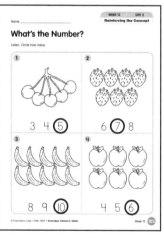

Day 3

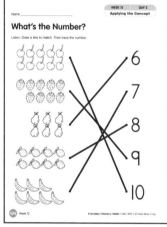

Day 4

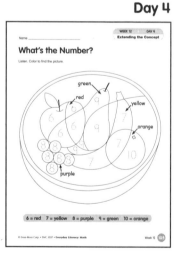

Week 13

Day 1

Day 2

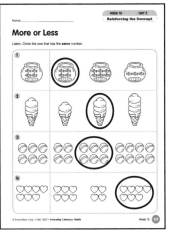

Day 3

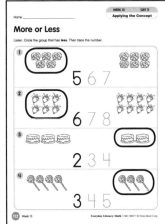

Day 4

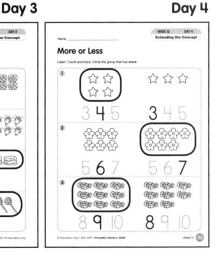

Week 14

Day 1

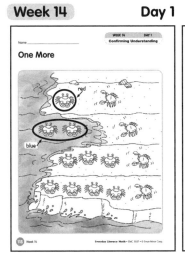

Day 2

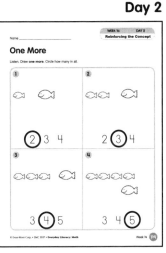

Day 3

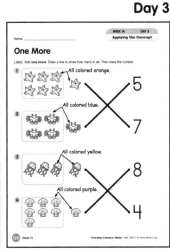

Day 4

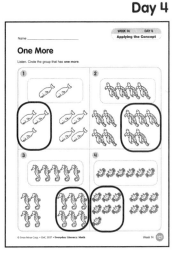

Week 15

Day 1

Day 2

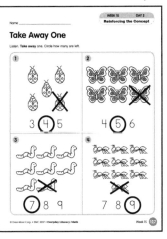

Day 3

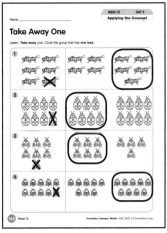

Day 4

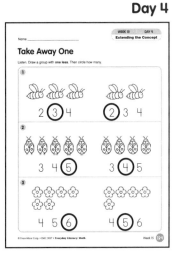

Week 16

Day 1

How Are They Different?

Day 2

How Are They Different?

Listen. Follow the directions.

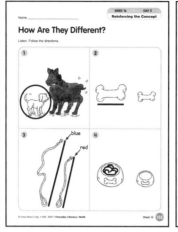

Day 3

How Are They Different?

Listen. Follow the directions.

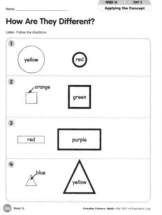

Day 4

How Are They Different?

Listen. Follow the directions.

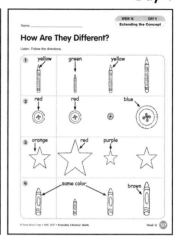

Week 17

Day 1

Let's Measure!

Day 2

Let's Measure!

Listen. Measure. Circle the correct answer.

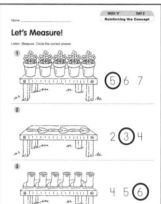

Day 3

Let's Measure!

Listen. Measure each flower using large paper clips.

Day 4

Let's Measure!

Listen. Follow the directions.

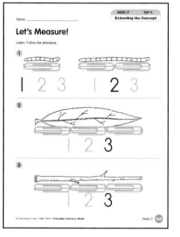

Week 18

Day 1

First in Line

Day 2

First in Line

Listen. Color the happy face for **yes**. Color the sad face for **no**.

Day 3

First in Line

Listen. Follow the directions.

Day 4

First in Line

Listen. Follow the directions.

Everyday Literacy: Math • EMC 3037 • © Evan-Moor Corp.